GOOD ENOUGH

GOOD ENOUGH

AUTOBIOGRAPHY OF A FORMER DRUG LORD: INCREDIBLY RICH BUT DESPERATELY MISERABLE

JOHAN TOET
CO-AUTEUR LINDA BRUINS SLOT

GOOD ENOUGH
Author: Johan Toet

Co-author: Linda Bruins Slot
Editing: Carolien Coppoolse
Translation: Joy Phillips and Michael Blommaert | thelanguagecollective.nl
Cover photo: Ruben Timman | www.nowords.nl
Layout: Vanderperk Groep | www.vanderperk.nl
Printing and printing assistance: Drukcase | www.drukcase.nl

The Bible verses quoted here are from the New King James Version (NKJV).

First print, 2019
Second edition, 2023

ISBN 978-90-8298-301-2

2019 © One in Him Foundation
www.oneinhimfoundation.com

CONTENTS

FOREWORD

Looking behind me, I saw a handsome, tanned face with sparkling eyes and a friendly smile. "What a nice guy! I'd like to have a chat with him later," I thought to myself.

"Hi, I'm Johan Toet." The big grin was back, and the sparkling, smiling eyes. Johan had just returned from a trip to Brazil with his wife Brenda, and they had driven here straight from Schiphol Airport because they were eager to meet me. From that very first moment, we felt a connection. Johan told me about their project and his passion to help the poorest of the poor in the slums of Brazil.

Since I share the same heart for the people, primarily living out my passion amongst the poorest of the poor in India, I recognized that drive in him. But we had even more in common. Freed, like him, from a dark past of drugs and demons that tortured me constantly, I wanted to shout it from the rooftops! I recognized that same inner drive in Johan.

But back then I didn't yet know how far Johan had come. I knew nothing of the emptiness, the cry for love and attention that had driven him so powerfully, even as a young boy. He thought he could fill that aching void by being macho and playing the big man, doing his best to get people to like him and accept him. He craved more and more to fill the bottomless pit of his heart. Johan had not yet learned that it was a dead-end road, and that nothing and no one could do that for him.

Now he's a fantastic ambassador for Christ, filled with fire and passion, unstoppably driven by the love of Jesus, the love he always longed for. That's why I love Johan so much, and consider it a great privilege to know him.

I'm sure you will also be inspired by this man's unimaginable and dramatic life story, as you discover how your life can change too. That's why Johan wrote this book. He wants nothing more than to see you discover that powerful, amazing love, just as he did. You too are Good Enough!

Highly recommended!

Jaap Dieleman – De Heilbode & Abba Child Care

PROLOGUE

It all flashed before me.
Every scene was horrible!
I felt their pain, fear, and sadness in my own body,
like a punch in the stomach.

What had I done?! Who had I become?!

With every fiber of my being I felt ashamed,
of everything:

the reason I was in prison, everything I had ever done,
truly everything.

It was so much, such a heavy burden.

Gradually my sobs turned into screams.
I beat myself on the chest and yanked my hair.
I yelled: "Ahhhhhhhh, why, why, why?!"

As I sat there crying and calling out, I seemed to be grabbed
by an invisible force. Before I knew it I was suddenly lying on
the ground.
What?
How did I get here?
What was going on?!

1

LIFE ON THE ROUGH SIDE OF TOWN

A police car cruised slowly down our street. Happened every day, so we weren't freaked out.

As the car passed, one of the guys started yelling. I couldn't understand what he was saying, but it sure wasn't anything like: "Hey handsome, doesn't your hair look slick today!"

The cruiser hit reverse and backed up to where we were. The window slowly rolled down. The tension grew.

The cop looked at each of us sternly, one at a time, and then said calmly, "If you're such a tough guy, step up and repeat what you just said." No one said a word.

This was my chance. I quickly stepped forward and spit at the cop, smack-dab in his face. "Filthy pig! Who do you think you are, you nasty jerkface?!"

Before he realized what was happening, I dashed off, darting between the others and away from the street. I obviously didn't want to get caught!

The cop searched and searched; after a while he gave up and drove on, and I rejoined the group. They loved it! "That Toet guy is a hardliner, for sure! The dude's as crazy as a loon!"

I was the top dog. That's why I did it.

DEATH AND LIFE ARE IN THE POWER OF THE TONGUE.

PROVERBS 18:21

This rundown old neighborhood was our home sweet home: Schilderswijk, one of the roughest parts of The Hague, notorious for violence, crime and corruption. Best spot in the city, as far as we were concerned. Around here something was always happening. The New Year's Eve bonfire always got lit on the street right outside our front door. The intense heat made the windows pop right out of their frames, and everybody loved it.

The fact that the neighbors' cars also caught fire didn't ruin our fun. Anything that would burn was tossed on the fire, and no cops dared to say a word; the whole neighborhood would have been up in arms if they tried.

That's how things were in Schilderswijk. Together we stood strong against anyone who was against us, anyone at all. I joined in from a very young age. The way we saw it, the police were our enemy, always, and nobody had ever seen anything.

School was stupid and boring. I really didn't feel like working for it, and often didn't bother to show up at all. Obviously, my grades were terrible. It wasn't that I wasn't smart enough; I just refused to do the work. Teachers who tried to boss me around were wasting their time. I hated that. They tried to punish me with lots of extra homework, but I didn't do it.

As soon as school was out, I would hang around on the streets. I didn't bother much with other kids my own age. The stuff they talked about was completely different from what I was into. Riiiiight, whatEVer, I thought, and went to hang out with the older boys. Seventeen or eighteen years old, most of them. I was a lot younger, but I did my best to keep up with them.

They taught me all sorts of things, but often enough they'd shut me up: "You little brat! Who said you could butt in here, kiddo?" Not so great, but it didn't stop me; I just tried harder to find other ways to earn their respect, to prove I really did fit in.

Thanks to my parents, I already had some status with the locals. Some families always did just a little bit better than others. The rest wanted the same for themselves, but it didn't always work out.

We were one of those families that kept managing to get more. One day my parents pulled into our street driving a new Mercedes with a big speedboat behind it. Everyone saw it: "Would you look at that! Well, well, check out what Johan's parents pulled off this time!"

So everywhere I went I heard people saying, "Hey, you know who his dad is?" That meant I was one of the guys, which was what I wanted more than anything.

When the boys headed over to the illegal squat, I went along. People were emptying out of the bars, and as usual my father was there. The whole neighborhood was there, standing on the bridge glaring at the squat. By then the police and the SWAT team had also arrived, ready to intervene if things got out of hand. Obviously, we were hoping they would.

Just then a squatter came cycling down the road, sporting a mohawk. You could have cut the tension with a knife, but the squatter calmly kept cycling along. How on earth could that punk just keep biking without anyone doing anything? But wait.
I walked out into the street, all alone. Behind me, a solid wall of thrill-seekers; to my left and right, the SWAT team blocking off the area. A punk on a bicycle in front of the building, and me in the middle of the road. There was a rock on the ground. Perfect.
I bent down, scooped up the rock, and threw it right at the squatter's skull, yelling: 'Filthy, dirty squatter, you ugly punk!'
My next insults were drowned out by the noise of the crowd. Officers rushed forward to grab me, but it was already too late. More stones flew through the air; everyone started yelling, howling, and running towards the building. Luckily I was fast and small, so I dashed through the crowd and hid in the bushes down the road.
The police horses trotted right past me; the officers poked long sticks into the bushes right next to where I was hiding, searching for me... But they didn't find me.

I stayed put, only returning to the guys after things had quieted down again.
"Wow, you're crazy, man, are you nuts? Did you see what happened?!"
Once again, I was the man! I had pulled it off. I started doing even more extreme stunts just to belong, and things were going pretty well.

Of course my father also heard that we were getting up to no good. He often had to pick me up from the police station because I had pulled something again. Each time I hoped he'd be proud. That's really why I did it. But no, he was always furious! He'd start shouting, pulling no punches, using local slang that was rude and crude and not fit to repeat.

He was rarely kind to me. In fact, he was hardly ever home at all – and when he was, he was drunk or grumpy. He never asked, "Hey, kid, what happened?"

No, he'd just call me all sorts of names and yell at me. Nothing was good enough. Even if I got home just half an hour late, I knew: brace for impact. So I'd head inside, sighing, shoulders slumped, my head hung low.

And then he'd unleash his anger on me. "Get lost, you good-for-nothing scum!" And so on. He shouted all the horrible curses he could think of.

He was trying to keep me on the straight and narrow, but his cruel words just made me sink lower. Sometimes I wished I'd never been born. To feel better about myself, I'd head out again to steal stuff and get up to mischief. It was a vicious cycle.

But my father wasn't exactly a saint himself. He stopped working the ships not long after I was born. "I abandoned my dream for my children's sake," he would often say. But then he'd spend days on end in the local bar.

He was on welfare, but he got most of his money from shady business like fencing stolen goods or running a bootleg TV channel broadcasting locally in The Hague. The whole neighborhood could watch porn and see movies that weren't available anywhere else. Local businesses paid for advertising time, and my mother even helped. They recorded her sitting behind our desk, like some kind of TV hostess. "Good evening, everyone, here's the show we have for you this evening."

My father almost always managed to outsmart the police. Everyone was afraid of him, too. Everywhere he went, in cafés or wherever, he would smash the place to pieces if he felt the situation called for it. He held a black belt 2nd Dan in karate and Teakwondo, so it was easy.

If he really couldn't sort stuff out with his fists, he'd just start shooting. Like everybody in our neighborhood, he had pistols and a shotgun in the house. That's how we dealt with our problems: yelling, making threats, fighting, and then shooting.

One afternoon, a car squealed around the corner into our street and pulled up right in front of our house. We soon figured out that the driver wasn't there for us. As it turned out, he had a bone to pick with the woman living in the downstairs apartment.

My dad with a machine gun

He started shouting up a storm and yelling curses at the big window on the corner. Then he got out of the car and threw a bottle of beer right through the neighbor's window. The sound of smashing glass echoed up and down the street. The man got back in his car and drove off. A little later he came back and started cursing again... And then he was off again.

By that time my mother had called my dad. As usual, he was in the café on the corner. He headed straight home, all his friends tagging along behind him. If someone's being rude to the neighbor lady, everybody comes along to lend a hand. That was just how we did things.

My father stood outside the house and said to my mom, "Bring it here." My mother knew exactly what he meant. She ran upstairs, got the shotgun out from under the bed, and tossed it to my father. He loaded the shotgun with a loud, clear click.

The car came back around again. My dad didn't hesitate for a second; he just shot out the windows in the back and side of the car. And it worked! That dude high-tailed it out of our street, driving as fast as he could. He must have thought: that man could just as well shoot me dead! And he might have been right.

My mother took the shotgun back upstairs, just in time, right before the police car pulled up. The officers got out of the car and came over to us. "We heard that shots were fired here."

The whole neighborhood put on their best innocent looks. "Shots fired? No, just a couple of firecrackers, that's all. Don't be silly! There's no shooting here. Do you see any weapons?"

The officers pointed to the street: "There's glass all over the place here. So how did it get there?"

"Oh sure, that's been there for weeks," one of the neighbors said, with a straight face. "Time for you to clean up that mess then, don't you think?"

The police couldn't do anything else, so they got back into their car. They had no evidence and no witnesses. The angry neighbor moved out the next day.

That's how my father took care of things. If someone was picking on me on the street, especially someone older, I'd tell my father. He'd head right over to ask what was going on, and beat the guy up if he had to. I had enormous respect for him, despite his harsh words.

Every now and then we'd see a different side of him, but only when he was really, really drunk.

"Boys, come take a seat," he'd say to me and my brother. We'd curl up on the sofa beside him while he listened to Neil Diamond. He'd sit with us and listen to a very long intro. "Beautiful, isn't it? So, so beautiful." He would hold us tight and say, all choked up, "I love you guys so much, you know. I really love you." And we'd be so happy, so incredibly happy.

When he was done, he'd say, "And now f*** off to your own room again," but we knew he was just kidding around. In our eyes, our father was really tough, a real man. Also an a**hole, but he was ours; he was our dad.

I knew how easily his mood could shift. That was part of who he was. That's why I was also so scared of him. He rarely hit us, but he could completely tear us apart with his words.

That's how things had been for him back home, too, my mother told me. My father came from a local family of seasoned alcoholics. Everyone was aggressive and swore a blue streak, like their lives depended on it. They had to fight hard to carve out a spot for themselves, and my dad got lots of hard knocks and not all that much love. I understood it. But that didn't do me much good when he was standing in front of me yelling.

There was always a sense of unease between the wonderful times and the normal moments – although it was never really normal.

When things were going well, it was because my father had made some money – or more accurately, "got lucky and managed to score a couple bucks." At times like that, we'd throw a big party, have everyone over; things would be good.

Or we'd go camping, I loved that. We had a little boat that we'd take out on the water. We went sailing and fishing for hours and hours. We really had a lot of fun together.

One afternoon he called us over and said in a hushed voice, "Come on, boys, take a seat. We need to talk to you." My mother was there too.

"Your father and mother are working on a thing. If we pull it off, we stand to make a whole lotta money. We could buy anything we want. You guys need to lie low for a bit, not pull any crazy stunts. If this works out, there's a ton of dough in it for us, and then we'll..."

We sat there listening breathlessly; it sounded so exciting! Yes, we promised to do our best.

But it wasn't easy. By that point I was already involved in some shady dealings and petty theft of my own.

As usual, something went wrong, and my father definitely couldn't handle that on top of everything else. He'd had a lot to drink, and someone called him out of bed early in the morning because I had stolen fifty bucks from a girlfriend.

A raging monster stormed out of his room! Furious, he yanked me out of my bed and hit me with a glass ashtray. The sharp edge sliced into my hand, leaving a deep cut.

Fast as I could, I pulled free from his grasp and ran out of the house. Things felt grim again after that.

Usually, I had really done what I was accused of and deserved to be punished. But my father's raging fury didn't put me on the straight and narrow – in fact, it did the exact opposite.

My mother could tell me a thousand times that I was everything to her, but I couldn't believe it... Even though she always did everything for us. She arranged everything, covered everything, solved everything. That's how she was.

But my father's words seemed to matter more. So often he would say, 'You're just a good-for-nothing, worthless nobody. There's not an ounce of good in you.' And I believed him.

I made sure to stay out of his way, and started hanging around in the street more and more. Scared to face his fury, scared to face his words. Trying to find ways to be good enough.

FOR MEN WILL BE LOVERS OF THEMSELVES, LOVERS OF MONEY, BOASTERS, PROUD, BLASPHEMERS, DISOBEDIENT TO PARENTS, UNTHANKFUL, UNHOLY, WITHOUT SELF-CONTROL AND HEADSTRONG.

2 TIMOTHY 3:2-4

2

SCHOOLING CUT SHORT

On the streets, I was the devil-may-care, tough kid who refused to listen to anyone and wasn't afraid of anything. I might have been the smallest kid in the group, but I still went all out. I was one of the guys! No one could stop me, not even the police. I was brave as a lion and completely crazy.

When I was with the guys, I felt ten miles tall. We always used to meet up at clubhouse Het Honk. We would get bored out of our skulls there, then come up with some pranks and get into all kinds of mischief just to get through the day. The older we got, the more serious the trouble we got into.

Every few weeks I ended up at the police station, picked up for stealing or fighting. That was our hobby, maybe even our life.

Every Thursday night, the guys and I used to go out into the town and seek out other groups of kids. We would go to the big department stores and walk out with armfuls of stolen clothes. At a fast food joint, we would order lots of food, and then refuse to pay for it. Of course that would end in a fight, and then we'd trash the place. And no one could stop us. There were just too many of us.

On other nights, we would head into more residential neighborhoods. I was small, so they put me to good use. Silver linings and all that. When we found a house we wanted to break into, the smallest opening was big enough for me to slip through. Who cared if the people were home or not? I was in and out like greased lightning. I would clean out the entire living room, even with the people who lived there still watching TV. We would jack cars off the street just because we felt like it. Or we would clean out a whole truck.

Our street had a store selling wholesale liquor and cigarettes, a salad distributor, and a candy factory. They were our favorite targets. They would load their trucks, and as soon as they headed back inside we would unload them again. And then we would have a big food fight with all those salads, because hey, what else could you do with it? The whole street and all the cars got covered in Russian salad!

The second we saw a chance to get some action, we just went for it. No one was afraid, me neither — it was a huge kick to see if we could get away with it. Times like that, I felt euphorically happy and incredibly proud. I thought I was fantastic, that I could handle anything the world could throw at me. And I often got away with it, too, even though I was guilty.

But not every time. Now and then I was unlucky and found myself in the wrong place at the wrong time. A girl from my class at school, 11 years old just like me, turned out to be pregnant, and I had had sex with her.

But I wasn't the only one. She had been with almost all the boys in the neighborhood: her own classmates, but also boys as old as eighteen. Since she was pregnant, she had to say who might have knocked her up. And yes, of course, Johan was one of the names on that list. It was true, I must confess. It was in the disabled toilet at school, nice and roomy, with all kinds of handholds to grab onto.

No one thought it was strange that we were already having sex. Even my parents didn't give me a hard time about that. When I brought another girl home, they'd just ask, "What's her name?" And then we'd go to my room and I would tell my parents not to bother us. And they wouldn't.

My mom wasn't particularly shocked by the situation, considering, so she went down to the station with me. After my talk with the police, I also had to go see the doctor. He asked me, "Have you ever ejaculated?" I looked at him, puzzled. I had no clue what he was talking about.

The doctor suggested that I should go into a little side room and try to make myself ejaculate. That's when my mom stepped in. She gave him a good talking-to, Hague-style: "Are you out of your bloody mind? Do you seriously believe that I'll let you tell my own child that he has to go and jerk off in some booth? Are you crazy or something? Get real, man!" And that was the end of that.

In the end, one of the older guys turned out to be the father. The girl had to get an abortion. A hard lesson learned, for me as well. Not least because I was expelled from school because of the whole situation.

Me and my dad in front of the café

Now what? I thought it would be great to become a chef and make all kinds of delicious foods. But apparently that wasn't something I could just start doing right away. First I had to do an orientation year at a vocational school, but I couldn't enroll until the start of the new school year.

I hadn't asked for it, but I wasn't sorry to discover that I didn't have to go to school for the rest of that school year. While everyone else was stuck in the classroom, I was free to wander the streets and see if I could make a couple bucks. I had myself a grand old time.

I had just turned thirteen when I had to go back to school. That took some getting used to, and not just because of the lessons. This school had a tradition: piglet hazing. The first-year 'piglets' were shoved into a muddy ditch. Ha, ha, so funny. Everybody gathered round to laugh and cheer.

No way was I playing along with that. The first person to touch me would get his nose broken, I decided.

Eventually it was my turn. A large group of people had gathered in a circle around me, near a huge puddle that had become a filthy mud pool after several days of heavy rainfall. Their plan was to roll me all the way through the puddle. Well, guess again.

Anybody who thought they could boss me around had better be prepared to get me up in their face. I didn't care if it was a cop or a class full of bigger boys. Who knows why; I just didn't. Maybe because of how my dad treated me.

As usual, I wasn't impressed. At the risk of getting my butt kicked, I said, "Which one of you is the strongest guy at this school?"

The boys started shoving each other jokingly, and a solidly built kid took a step forward. He stared at me intensely, but I could see a nervous twitch on his face. It was all or nothing; my reputation was on the line.

Squaring my shoulders, my head held high, I walked up to him and said, "Listen up, pal." When the boy came closer to hear what I wanted to say I headbutted him in the nose and followed up with my fists.

He reeled for a moment, yelping from the unexpected pain. Blood trickled down his face and dripped into the puddle, making it look even more dramatic. Everyone started hollering and whistling and calling out and laughing!

Meanwhile, I walked up to the guy who was covered in his own blood and whispered in his ear: "If you and I join up, we can take on the entire school and rule this place." He nodded, holding a hand to his nose. I did it! I had it made! No one was going to mess with me anymore.

Through a friend of mine, I had managed to get my hands on some hash, so my new buddy and I started selling it. We cut up a chunk of hash into smaller pieces and hid them in other people's lockers. Our business was doing well, and there was plenty of demand.

I spent my school year dealing drugs, hitting on girls and getting into trouble. I had a great time at that school.

When the year was finally over, I got to choose if I wanted to stay at this school or if I still wanted to switch to a serious cooking school. Of course I chose the latter.

The François Vatel cooking school was pretty fancy; things there were different from what I was used to. No more loafing around, and definitely no more dealing dope.

Because I enjoyed it so much, I took it more seriously and worked harder. I loved learning how to cook, making pastries and baking bread rolls. Still, even at this school things went completely off the rails. But that wasn't all my fault.

First of all, they made a fuss about my long hair. According to school regulations I was supposed to cut it short. How about 'No!'? My hair was my identity. That was the first confrontation, but they did let me stay.

Of course I made mistakes now and then, and I wasn't always done on time. Still, I enjoyed it and really wanted to become a chef. But apparently that was not meant to be.

I spent three days working hard at putting together a chocolate house. It was really, really fun to do. But it took me a bit too long to finish it, so I was late handing it in.

When I entered the classroom, I saw beautiful chocolate houses on all the tables. I was super proud of my house; it really was beautiful and I had made it all by myself. But I was late for class. Apparently I had been late one time too many and the teacher was all done being lenient. He looked at me and said, "Go and see the principal."

Astonished, I looked at my house and back at the teacher. "So I'm not allowed to hand it in?"

He was adamant: "No. You're too late."

It felt like something inside me was exploding. I gave him one more chance. "So you're telling me I'm not allowed to hand it in?"

All done being patient with me, he raised his voice. "Didn't you hear me? Go and see the principal now!"

"OK." And I completely lost it. Bam! I threw the house on the floor, shattering it to pieces at his feet. The entire class held their breath, waiting to see what would happen.

But I wasn't done yet. "If I'm not allowed to hand it in, then no one is allowed to hand it in." Like a raging bull, I stomped around the classroom and BAM! smashed all the other chocolate houses. And then I went to the principal's office.

My parents happened to be there already for something else. "Oh, that's a coincidence," the principal said. "Have you been sent out of class again?'

"No, I just had to be here," I said innocently. "All right, so you were sent out of class again."

It didn't take long for them to decide. "We've run out of options with this boy."

I had to start looking for something else to study. I was really bummed about that, since I loved cooking school. What could I do next?

My brother worked as a painter four days a week and went to school one day a week. I could do that too, but it meant I would have to start looking for a job for four days a week. But what kind of job? I had no clue, because I had no skills. And honestly, I didn't really feel like working. Still, I started going to that school.

On the very first day, I joined my brother in class, with maybe thirty students in total. A woman with red hair and a red face entered the classroom. What a horrible, creepy person!

Turned out she was the school principal. Talking in a prissy voice, she said: "The next person to get sent out of class will be expelled from school immediately." There had already been a couple of incidents, apparently, which was why she felt the need to make such a ridiculous threat. Then she walked out of the classroom again on her high heels. Man, was she stuck up!

Next to me, I heard my brother mutter under his breath: "Well, that's just great." Just an ordinary comment. Very calm and quiet.

"OK, you," the teacher said to my brother, "get out."

My brother looked at him in shock. He had never been sent out of class before; he had really never done anything bad at all! In fact, the way my father treated us had made him very shy and insecure; he had even developed a stutter. He stammered, "Yes, but then I'll lose my job."

"Get out!" the teacher said, even louder this time.

I was not about to let this happen! I jumped up from my chair, ran up to the teacher and punched him. My brother came and stood next to me, backing me up. I hissed at the teacher, "The second you leave the school building..." and I pulled my finger across my throat in a slashing motion. I couldn't have been clearer.

Me and my brother ran away from there, heading outside. We laughed and laughed as we ran, but my brother sounded worried, saying, "Still too bad about my job."

"Oh well, it'll be all right," I said carefree. I couldn't have cared less; I had nothing to lose. We arrived home and said nothing to my mom and dad about what had happened.

But as luck would have it, the cops were at our door a little later. "The teacher felt threatened and has filed charges."

That was the end of my school career.

FOR THIS SORT ARE THOSE WHO CREEP INTO HOUSEHOLDS AND MAKE CAPTIVES OF GULLIBLE WOMEN LOADED DOWN WITH SINS, LED AWAY BY VARIOUS LUSTS.

2 TIMOTHY 3:6

3

FROM BAD TO WORSE

My dad made me go out to find a job. As I said before, I had a big problem with authority, so that went wrong from the get-go. On my first day at a hardware store, the business manager barked at me, "Get to work, and make sure you're done with that by this afternoon."

"Sure," I said obediently, but the first thing I did was have a look around to see what I might be able to steal. Paid close attention to the alarm code, and in we went! After barely two days working at that job, we robbed the safe that night.

It was simply a part of me, it came along on my path; that was just the way it went. All the guys I hung around with were also out on the streets all day. Their fathers were probably in the drug scene or involved in some other illegal business. I also hung out with lots of Travelers and other people living in trailer parks, even outside my neighborhood. That was our life. Stealing and cheating, that was how we did things.

Girls were also part of that life. I regularly had girlfriends, but by the time I was fifteen I had really fallen in love for the first time. I was completely head over heels; my entire life revolved around her and only her. I had never felt like that before. Life was perfect!

Unfortunately, it did not last long. Out of the blue, she suddenly told me that her parents wouldn't let her see me anymore. Apparently, I wasn't good enough for them. That was the end of it; what we had was over. My heart broke into a million pieces.

In my frustration, I beat up two guys on my way home, and twisted their bikes around a streetlight. Just hearing her name brought my world crashing down. Completely heartbroken, I locked myself away in my room.

After a few weeks, I decided to go out again, although I looked miserable. "Hey man, come here," a couple of my friends said after a while.

I followed them into the bathroom. One of the guys shook some white powder onto my hand. "Snort this! That will cheer you up again."

At that point I had never tried cigarettes or alcohol before, and I had no idea what the powder was. I took one snort, and immediately I was sold. The stuff burned for a second, but then my nose felt numb. A drop slithered down my throat and my entire mouth went numb. My heart started beating faster and my eyes opened wide.

It was almost like I rose above myself. All the sorrow, all the pain was gone. Everything was okay; in fact, I felt amazing! Even more guts, even more sass, everything was going great that evening. The whole night long I rode the edge.

Full of confidence, I immediately hit on another girl; I felt like I could take on the world. And all of that just from one snort. "Wow, I want to try that again!"

So I did. At first only on weekends, one snort at a time. I even managed to get home on my own.

But pretty soon that didn't cut it anymore. So I also started snorting cocaine on weekdays. Then me and my buddies would hang out on the beach or at the clubhouse for the day. That's how I started using more and more, taking more at a time, and needing it more often.

Eventually, my focus was entirely on cocaine. It was my escape from the reality of a life where I couldn't do much of anything and didn't feel like I was good enough. I still didn't drink or do other crazy stuff; I only used coke... Lots and lots of coke.

Because I needed more, I also needed to find a way to get more money. More than I could make just from petty theft and burglary. So I started dealing drugs, more and more.

One day my father came to me, stood over me menacingly, and asked: "I heard from a couple of my buddies that you've been using cocaine. Is that true, yes or no?" Sure, I had snorted coke with my dad's buddies in a night club. In fact, they were the ones who gave me the coke! And then ratted me out to my father.

What was I supposed to say? I didn't want to spill the beans on his friends, or get myself into trouble. I knew my father well enough.

So I said, "No, I'm not."

"OK. Because if you are, I'll break your nose, you know that." I was still afraid of him, and I sure didn't want to get punched in the nose. He repeated, "I didn't think you were, but I'd be very upset if you did."

I denied it again, but it bothered me. A couple of days later I went ahead and told him it was true. "But I did it with your buddies, Dad."

He didn't care about that at all. He was furious. "Then why did you lie to me? I knew I couldn't trust you." He didn't say, "Hey, I'm glad you were honest with me." No, he was all up in my face about it.

From then on, he was even meaner to me than before. I seriously couldn't do anything right in his eyes. He kept saying that he didn't want that life for me, but of course I didn't understand. All I could see was a furious dad who got into all sorts of trouble himself, but yelled at me every chance he got. The more he called me a useless bum, the more I was willing to do anything to prove I really was somebody.

Something was born in me then, an ego so big that I could already see myself standing on that hill with all of those kingdoms – like Jesus once stood next to Satan – even though I had nothing at all. If I had to make a deal with the devil to be somebody, then I'd do it.

I got more and more involved in drug dealing, getting bigger all the time and earning more and more money. Every time I earned some money, I suddenly had a lot of friends. That was my goal, especially when it was the older guys who suddenly considered me good enough to hang around with.

Thankfully, I also had a real buddy, we called him Quiet Guy, who was almost always with me, and not just when I had made some money. He also had my back if there were problems. I was extremely loyal to him; I was willing to do anything to show I was worthy of his friendship.

Nose also became my buddy, after we made a daring getaway together. The pigs were in hot pursuit after a fight with the local police. They were sweeping our streets, picking up suspects: if we hadn't made it out in time, we would have been caught red-handed. Nose and I ran for our lives, giggling hysterically as we high-tailed it out of there. We had an instant click.

We stole a car together and raced it all over town. We went completely wild, snorting coke and getting into all sorts of craziness. Eventually we plowed the car right into a row of other cars, and then took off again, roaring with laughter.

I hung out with those two guys off and on, and almost inevitably we'd start snorting coke, partying and stealing stuff.

One night Quiet Guy and I went over to the campground. I had just bought an old Ford Taunus for five hundred guilders, an automatic instead of a stick shift, and I drove it like it was a Ferrari. Since I was barely seventeen years old and didn't have a driver's license, I preferred to let someone else drive if we were going to take the highway. Once we arrived at the campground with a bag of coke, we took more and more until it stopped being fun.

Quiet Guy got a spoon and started mixing some coke and ammonia in it. Then he heated the spoon until the mixture turned oily. He saw me watching in fascination and said, "This isn't for you, mate." He poured the oil on a piece of foil and started heating it, using a pipette to inhale the smoke coming off the foil and then exhaling it again. With every hit, he grew quieter and quieter; he just sat there smoking.

Meanwhile, I was only allowed to watch. Eventually I grew tired of that and said, "Give me a puff too!"

Without speaking a word, he continued to shake no with his head, but I wouldn't have been Johan if I took no for an answer, so I started digging into him: "Whose coke are you smoking right now? That's mine, right? And you won't even let me try it? Man, you are so full of yourself! What an ego!"

After trying and trying to talk him into it, I managed to get him to give in, and he handed me the foil. Just like I saw him do it, I tried to inhale some smoke, but the only thing I managed to do was drool on the foil through the pipette, making everything sizzle and pop, doing just about anything except getting any smoke in my lungs.

Quiet Guy was really cracking up by that point, falling over with laughter. It all took way too much time, in my opinion, and I didn't like that. So I went back to snorting. Even so, something inside of me was still curious about how it would feel, so I gave it one more try.

This time I took it real slow. I sucked the air in hard and felt the smoke filling my lungs. Immediately I was hit by a euphoric feeling that was even better than snorting coke.

I had developed a taste for it now. Before I knew it, my hands were blackened from the scorched foil, I had a burn on my thumb from hours flipping my lighter, and my lips were so numb that it felt like I had been kissing an iceberg all night.

The night had come and gone, and we were almost out of coke, so I decided to score some easy money. I kicked the door in at some supermarket and went in. I scooped up all the cigarettes and coffee I could carry into trash bags and loaded them into my car.

Then I went and picked up Quiet Guy to help me. We sold the stuff in The Hague, unloading it to my uncle, who was always up for a shady deal. He was neck-deep in all sorts of illegal business, and also had something going in restaurants and cafés. All of my uncles were crooks with an established rep in The Hague, and no one messed with them. I looked up to them and wanted to impress them.

With the money from our haul, we bought a bag of coke and went back to the campground and smoked it until we ran out again. That was how I spent my life: stealing, hustling and smoking.

By then, it was the middle of summer and the nights never seemed to end; something was happening around every corner. I enjoyed life to the fullest and had an insatiable hunger for money.

I was in regular contact with Fatty, who came from a Roma family. He was someone my dad knew, and we'd go hustle everyone and their mom together. He was well into his forties and already had a family, while I was barely seventeen years old. He was a real criminal, so I loved that he wanted to hang out with me. Of course I understood it was because I always managed to earn money and wanted to share it with everyone, but I didn't care.

One night I had a brainstorm: there was this guy who always carried around a lot of cash, which he would flash in the bar so he could brag about it. But when he was wearing a tracksuit, he never carried that nice fat wallet with him — so all that cash would probably be at his house.

Fatty and I got into the car and drove to the bar where the guy liked to hang out. When we arrived, I spotted the guy at a table, and yes indeed, he had his tracksuit on. We took off right away and headed over to his house. "Wait here," I said to Fatty. He was pretty heavy-set, so I didn't think he'd be able to climb through a bathroom window without drawing suspicion.

Once I reached the house, I quickly scoped out the scene to check if I could see anyone. Just when I was about to get a metal flowerpot to smash in the window, I spotted an open window. Awesome, such great service!

Like a greased monkey, I climbed inside and felt around for the light switch, groping in the dark. The second I found it I switched on the light. Almost like I was drawn to it, I walked straight to a drawer and opened it. And there it was: the wallet full of money! I grabbed it and quickly stashed it in my waistband.

Then I climbed back out through the window, walked back to the car, got in and said, "Let's drive! We're going on a holiday!'

Fatty looked at me incredulously. "You've only been gone for, like, two minutes!"
I slapped his shoulder and started laughing.

"Come on, dude, drive faster! The wallet was just lying there in a drawer. He's such an idiot! I just knew it!"

After driving for a while, we stopped and counted the fat roll of banknotes. The adrenaline was racing through my body. Seven thousand guilders! We were ecstatic; that was a great haul for such a short run.

From my share I bought a secondhand Opel Senator, a big, luxurious cruiser. Now I was really the bomb.

I still didn't have my license, unfortunately, so it was usually Quiet Guy who drove. We raced that beast all across the country, and we even took a trip all the way to Spain. What a rush! We snorted and partied; this summer was the best.

Or was it? One evening, I had a girl in my car and was talking too much, playing it too macho, and I completely totaled my car. The rest of the money went straight up my nose, so I had to start all over again.

4

MY FIRST TIME IN PRISON

Something had happened to my father. Suddenly he was all about God, even talking about it in the bar. His mates all laughed and made fun of him. "There he is again! Hey, you're not gonna be some kind of preacher, right?" He got sick of it and stopped going to the bar; he quit seeing all his old friends.

Soon after, he had a 'moment with God', as he called it. He couldn't stop crying and felt a sense of freedom. I didn't understand it, but I did think it was extraordinary. It was noticeable that he was a lot calmer, but other than that he didn't really change all that much.

He just kept sitting on the couch, watching TV and forcing other people to listen to his opinions. Everything still had to go exactly the way he wanted. He quit drinking, but started smoking weed instead.

He made new friends who were also constantly smoking weed. They were often at his place; he liked it that way. I did have a better relationship with him by then, and we had more fun too – but that all depended on his mood on any given day. He was still very belligerent about his opinions, so we still tiptoed around him. And I didn't tell him anything about my business.

To get money, I sold everything I could get my hands on. I didn't care what it was. From fake Rolexes to knock-off tracksuits with illegal logos: anything that crossed my path, I'd sell. Wholesalers were great, obviously. I would regularly break into the big box stores and snatch anything worth reselling: booze, coffee, diapers, cigarettes. I could always 'earn' some money that way.

Occasionally I'd get caught. Then I'd spend a couple of days or max a week in a holding cell at the police station. Sometimes I could get off with just a fine, sometimes a suspended sentence, but in the end I always just went home again. Of course something was bound to go wrong eventually.

HE WHO SOWS INIQUITY WILL REAP SORROW.

PROVERBS 22:8

On New Year's Eve we always burned things: old cars, tires, anything flammable. Close to where we lived was an abandoned building full of car tires. Other people had already broken in a couple of times to steal some car tires to toss on the bonfire.

At a certain point we decided, "Let's just burn the whole building down. It's gonna be fun!" One of the guys lived nearby, so we would have a front-row seat when the fire department got there.

Of course it was me again who said: "I'll do it," and I headed into the building with a jerrycan. A jet of flame scorched off part of my hair and my tracksuit melted in places, but it was all worth it to me. I climbed out through the window and we watched the fire from a distance.

A few days after New Year's Eve, I got arrested. I seriously had no clue what I had done wrong this time, so I thought I would be there and gone in no time.

Unfortunately, it turned out to be more serious than I thought. I hadn't known that there was a petrol tank under that building with two thousand liters of petrol. It could easily have caused a major explosion. That's why they didn't let me off easy this time: I got fifteen months in jail. That was serious! I was still just seventeen years old.

They sent me to juvie, De Sprang juvenile detention in the coastal town of Scheveningen, and I ended up in First Offenders, the department for kids who were going inside for the first time. Intense, such a long sentence, but juvie itself wasn't that bad, thankfully. We all had our own cell with a TV; it was a nice setup.

I knew most of the guys in there. This was Scheveningen, my home turf. We had a good time together and the months passed pretty fast. We also had to attend a program with support groups, re-education classes, nonsense like that. Like, we had to learn how to write an application letter if we wanted to apply for a job. Like any of us would ever use that skill set.

Once in a while my girlfriend slipped me some coke, passing it to me when we kissed. One time she was holding it in a tiny plastic bag in her mouth. When she passed it to me, the bag ripped open. After that I jerked around so much that I looked like some kind of rock star! It was a miracle I made it through inspection after visiting hours.

There was a small hole in my wall that I used to pass rolling papers and cigarettes to my buddy in the cell next to me. Sometimes we'd sit in our cells side by side, spacing out on coke together. Not bad! Even though I didn't smoke weed myself, I did occasionally smuggle in some hash. One day, Nose brought a huge chunk of hash with him on his visit, 40 grams.

"Where am I supposed to hide that?" I asked him. He laughed so hard he got tears in his eyes, and I knew I was in big trouble. No, not up my butt, no way! Exit only, do not enter. So I just stuffed it down my briefs.

During inspection by the guards, I had to drop my pants, and I realized that the chunk of hash was sticking to my scrotum. Good, I got lucky this time! Then they told me to squat. I heard a thud. The hash fell off and lay there on the ground, looking pathetic. The guard said, "What do we have here?"

Looking behind me with an astonished look on my face, I said, "Well, I never! How did you manage to do that?" They laughed, and I was kept in my cell for three days.

After a few months in Scheveningen, I was transferred to Vught, a short-stay prison for people with sentences less than two years. My cell was in the income ward, and I worked there for a month or two before I was allowed to go to another ward where I could get more privileges, like cooking and rec time.

My days were terribly boring. At 7 a.m. my radio alarm clock went off, and every morning I heard the same record: 'Why Worry' by the Dire Straits. Why worry? Easy for them to say! I was stuck in there and they got to go home at the end of the day.

At 8 a.m., they brought me super-intelligent work to do: they gave me a couple of crates filled with screws and boards and plastic caps, and I had to assemble them into TV antennas. Every single day.

Sometimes they'd give me pieces of paper that I had to fold into paper cones to cover plants. Just fascinating. We had to make thousands of them.

All day long I sat in my cell doing things like that, with an hour outdoors once a day. It was really a hard time.

Meanwhile, my parents were offered a different house. My father was sick of the neighborhood. Since he had stopped drinking, he didn't have the same ties to the area, so he wanted to get out of there.

They decided to keep their old house so I could rent it. Looked like it was time to start living on my own. Once I got out, I would have a place of my own. Fantastic! That meant my brother would live right

FOR ALL THAT IS IN THE WORLD — THE LUST OF THE FLESH, THE LUST OF THE EYES, AND THE PRIDE OF LIFE.

1 JOHN 2:16

next to me and we could walk right into each other's houses through the balcony at the back. At least that was a ray of hope for me in those dark times.

My parents decided to start taking care of two little girls. Their mother was a drug addict and prostitute, and couldn't take care of them anymore. My mother was delighted to take them in. I suddenly had two sisters in my life. It took some getting used to, but I was also happy for my parents.

Finally I got a temporary pass and could spend a weekend at home! I had been looking forward to that for so long after the long months inside.

Fortunately, I had a girlfriend on the outside, so I was planning to have a great time that weekend. We agreed to spend two days together. After months of going without, I was really looking forward to that.

I was so happy to see everyone again, and go to my own house. First I walked to my brother's place. It was so wonderful to be there and laugh together again. Some other people were there, including his new girlfriend. She was cute and funny.

"Hi, I'm Johan," I said, and plopped on the couch, next to her. She said her name was Sandra, and we started shooting the breeze. It was nice just to be around regular people, and to be flirting with a blonde chick who was constantly checking me out. I felt on top of the world.

When my brother went into the kitchen, I followed him and asked, "Are you guys in a serious relationship?"

He laughed and said, "No, man, I was just about to dump her. It was just for fun. You know how it is, right?"

All right then, that's great.

"Do you mind if I take a shot?"

"Hey, that's what brothers are for, right?" he replied, and we roared with laughter. Man, I was really feeling lucky today, and I had only been out of prison for an hour. In good spirits, I went back into the room and started a full charm offensive. Of course it worked.

Before I knew it, she was sitting on my lap in the living room of my new house. Then we ended up in the American-style bed that my parents had given me, a cheesy thing with a red velvet headboard, a built-in radio and mirrors along the back. This was the life; I was the man.

It was late when I finally fell asleep, and I was startled awake the next morning by someone ringing the doorbell over and over, and rattling the mail flap in the front door. Who could that be, and why so early?

Annoyed, I looked out the window. To my dismay, I saw my date standing in front of my door, all dressed up, looking sexy and ready to party this weekend. Oh no! I had planned this weeks ago, fantasized about it, and was really looking forward to it... and I had completely forgotten.

The bell kept on ringing and the door kept rattling. From my window, I looked at her, then at my bed where Sandra looked back at me, sleepy and surprised.

What should I do?! Should I let her stand there at my door? Should I send away the chick who was in my bed and break her heart, after my brother had already dumped her yesterday? What a dilemma, so early in the morning! How could everything go from so good to so bad in no time?

Sandra asked what was going on.

"Sorry, I completely forgot my date with my girlfriend... What should I do?"

Sweetly, she answered, "Well, who do you really like?" Good point.

The last time I went on a date with that girl, it hadn't worked out the way I wanted; I had only planned another date with her because I didn't have a better alternative. But I felt a connection to this girl lying in my bed.

"If I let her go, will you stay with me all weekend?"

"Love to," she said.

Good, I decided, I'll ignore the doorbell. She kept up for a little while longer, but then I saw her walking down the street in her high heels, looking furious.

Sunday arrived sooner than I wanted it to and I couldn't stand to go back to prison so soon already. I didn't want to lose this feeling of happiness or the attention I was getting. After talking it over with my parents, I decided to take a gamble: I wouldn't report back in.

Life was smiling on me again, everything was going my way, I was earning money and having fun. Meanwhile, I had also started snorting coke again. Every weekend I would pick up a couple of baggies from one uncle and then go to my other uncle's club. Practically the entire underworld of The Hague hung out there. Everybody knew each other, so it was often tons of fun with a lot of crazy stuff going on.

It was Saturday night and the joint was packed. Together with my brother and his new girl, and my latest catch, Sandra, I felt pretty much at home.

At the end of a fun evening, as usual we were among the last few people still there. A guy came up to us and said something unintelligible, with a big smile. When I asked him to repeat what he said, I found out he was insulting my girl.

Without thinking, I punched him right in the nose. Quick as lightning, my brother kicked him in the face, and then my uncle jumped on the guy and kept whaling on him. The guy turned out to be from some other notorious local family, and before we knew it we had started a small war. Fortunately, we proved too strong for them and things calmed down again.

Our family were all crooks, boozers and fighters, violent and easily agitated, and we all wanted just one thing – money, lots and lots of money. We might not get along all that well with each other, but when it came down to it, we always had each other's back.

Just like that night. Somehow that made me proud to be part of this family. I was on the run from the law, so I wasn't entitled to any welfare benefits, but I wanted to live my life however I pleased, and keep snorting coke whenever I wanted it. That meant I needed to pull out all the stops to make lots of money.

Bigger crimes were looking more attractive all the time. I tried to come up with all sorts of schemes to get my hands on money, and I was willing to take increasingly drastic steps to get it. The urge to prove myself was huge; it was all about my ego.

One night, me and my brother and another buddy were driving through the slums of The Hague. We had some coke with us and an illegal weapon, and we were on our way to my uncle's club.

Suddenly the cops blocked our car from all sides and pulled us out of the car. Apparently, some guys in a similar car had done something and we were being arrested for it. Of course they found the baggies of coke and the gun in the car.

This was bad news for me. I still had ten weeks left on my sentence, and I really didn't want to go back to prison. With a quick jerk I pulled myself free and started running, so fast that I could hear the cops cursing and shouting far behind me.

On the other side of the street, I could see police cars coming my way, their sirens wailing. As the cars reached me, I pivoted unexpectedly and ran the other way. With my hands cuffed on my back, I kicked against doors to see if any were unlocked, but no such luck. Thinking quickly, I ducked under a parked truck and kept as quiet as a mouse. Adrenaline was coursing through my body; excitement always gave me a rush.

The cops walked along the street, cursing and scanning the area with their flashlights. I could hear them clearly, but they couldn't see me and walked on past. "Man, that guy is fast! S***, we lost him!"

Silently, I laughed at them. It seemed I had managed to get away squeaky clean. I began to feel a little calmer – but suddenly the entire street was lit up by bright floodlights, and I could hear dogs barking and sniffing. That wasn't good!

Sure enough, close to me I heard a dog start barking, and before long it bit my leg. "Ow!" I yelled. It hurt a lot, and I rolled out from under the truck. "Get that f***ing dog away from me, I'm here, I'm here! Get it off me!"

"Stand still, you little punk!" the cops shouted. To their shame, they had almost lost a seventeen-year-old boy in handcuffs, with thirty cops around him. They were relieved that they had managed to apprehend me after all.

At the police station, they found out why I was running from them. My brother and buddy were released again, and I was sent back to Vught prison. My girl decided to wait for me, and I served out the rest of my sentence in peace.

DO NOT BE DECEIVED, GOD IS NOT MOCKED; FOR WHATEVER A MAN SOWS, THAT HE WILL ALSO REAP.

GALATIANS 6:7

5

TAXI DRIVERS AND A PIZZA DELIVERY GUY

After I got out of prison again, I went out even more often and used even more coke, sometimes snorting it and other times smoking it.

Sandra and I weren't doing too well. We were getting into more and more arguments, and more and more I started doing things in secret. Sometimes I would sell some of our stuff and when I earned a bit of money again, I would buy it back. I lied to her time after time, because the coke was stronger than my love for her.

Regularly she would ask me, "Have you been using again?" I always denied it, even though I was sure she could see right through me. After the umpteenth time, she was so sick and tired of getting hurt that we split up. The coke had shattered our relationship.

By that point I had moved to another street and could do whatever I wanted. No more girlfriend checking up on me or parents getting in my way. I was completely free to drown myself in anything, and by that point I was a serious cokehead.

At the dealer's house where I got my coke, I saw someone smoking it off a glass. Basing, it was called. He shared a drag with me and I was immediately gone. From the tips of my toes to the ends of my hair, it felt like one huge orgasm. I wanted to feel that way all the time!

I couldn't stop thinking about it all day long and I wanted to use it as much as I could. I chased and I chased, but I couldn't seem to get the high that I was looking for, so I chased even more. As a result, I sometimes did incredibly stupid things. But very profitable. And often so easy.

For instance, a lot of taxi drivers in The Hague were fooled simply by wrapping a package of flour in tape. Obviously a brick of drugs, anyone could see that. Hurriedly, I would climb into a taxi with my package clearly visible. I'd lean forward and say, "I need to go to Den Bosch, but I first need to stop by a store in the city center to pick up a test kit."

Downtown was a drug house with two entrances. You could go in on one side and go out again on the other. On the same street was also a store that sold everything connected with drug use, from scales to baggies, packages and pipes. Every taxi driver knew about it.

The driver would hear what I had to say. He would check out the merchandise on my lap, and almost every taxi driver I met was a little bent and eager to make a little extra money.

Once we arrived at that particular street, I would get out and ask him if I could leave my merchandise in the cab for a bit. "I'll be right back." I'd slide the fake brick of coke under my seat. A minute or two later, I would walk back and say, "S***, man, I left my wallet at home. I'm about to get fifty thousand guilders. If you can spot me a couple hundred, I'll give you an extra thousand once we get there." The driver would get dollar signs in his eyes.

It never failed. I'd get anything between two and three hundred bucks off them, then I'd walk into the drug house, buy some coke, and walk out on the other side. The taxi driver had gained a package of flour and lost a couple hundred bucks.

The cabbies were apparently so humiliated that they were afraid to tell anyone what had happened, so I was able to keep going for a really long time.

Unfortunately, one day the jig was up. One cabby did talk – and then they all figured out how many taxi drivers I had scammed. They found my house, and when I wasn't home they completely trashed the place. Later they came back again, when I was home. Suddenly furious cabbies surrounded my front door.

"Come on, let's just kick the door in!" I heard them yelling to each other.

High as a kite on coke, I stood behind the front door, holding a Smith & Wesson .357 Magnum that I had stolen a couple of days ago, and I kept it pointed at the front door. If anyone got in through that door, I was going to start blasting away immediately. They were not going to get me, and I decided I would take a couple of them to the grave along with me.

My heart was pounding in my throat from the adrenaline! But then I heard sirens. Before long the cops removed the cabbies from the doorway. The police didn't even knock on my front door.

Clearly, I had a guardian angel on my shoulder. If there was a God, He had just prevented a massacre.

By then I had used so much coke at such a young age that my body had nearly reached its breaking point. The pain in my kidneys and lower back got progressively worse, until it became unbearable. When I went to the hospital for a check-up, I was admitted immediately; I turned out to have cirrhosis of the liver and the onset of kidney failure. That was serious.

My parents were called and came to the hospital, concerned about me. Apparently, I had about as much stamina as an old man; the doctors were pessimistic. They operated on me, and removed my appendix too, just to be sure. The general anesthetic alone was almost too much for me.

I really felt sick. One night I called my father from the hospital and asked him to come. Even though he didn't have a driver's license, he arrived in no time: he ran the whole way! I was deeply touched: my father really did love me.

After about a week I felt better again. The doctors wanted me to stay in the hospital, but I snuck out to look for coke. I took a taxi again, this time from a different company.

I had already sold the driver on my scam, and he had even handed over some money, but before I could get out of the cab, we were pulled over and surrounded by police officers pointing their pistols at me. They arrested me and put me in handcuffs.

Down at the station, the pain had become agonizing, since I obviously hadn't recovered completely. After a couple of days they let me go again because they didn't have a shred of evidence on me. The cabbies had handed their money over to me themselves. It was just flour, nothing illegal about that.

That was how I slipped through the cracks of the system, getting away with what I was doing. Occasionally they would lock me up for a short time, for possession of an illegal firearm or some other small stuff. I'd barely be out of court for one case before I was arrested again for something else. It wasn't usually all that bad, but sometimes it really got out of hand.

I had been smoking coke with various people for days on end. We were completely spaced out and had barely eaten anything; just the coke was enough for us. When we eventually got hungry, one of the girls suggested that we could just order pizza and not pay for it.

"Man, then we might as well take his money too," my buddy suggested. Just take his money and send the dude on his way. That sounded stupid but simple. It seemed like a perfectly good plan to me, though I didn't really get what it would involve.

The pizza guy came in and put the pizza on the table. I wanted to say to him, "My man, we don't have any money, so we'll pay the bill later. Just go away."

But that wasn't how it went, unfortunately. To my surprise and dismay, my buddy flipped out and started smacking the delivery guy around. His glasses were on the floor in pieces, and he had a broken finger and a broken nose. That wasn't the plan! "Why did you hit that guy? You really shouldn't have done that."

My buddy was just as upset as I was. "Yeah man, sorry, I started flipping out. I thought: what if he got aggressive or something?"

"What do you mean aggressive, he's outnumbered! He was just supposed to give us his money and leave."

But that wasn't what went down, so we had a big problem. The neighbors had heard everything and immediately called the police. In no time a patrol car pulled up outside. It was my house, and there was nowhere for me to go. We were completely made because of something incredibly stupid.

In a desperate attempt to escape, I climbed up on the roof, but it was no use. They sent dogs onto the roof via the ladder of a fire truck. Considering my previous experiences with dogs, I surrendered and climbed back into the house. There I was again: down on the floor, cuffed up and cussed out. I was all too familiar with that tune.

Since I had been in prison before, I was sentenced to thirty months for the robbery. The guy who actually hit him got twelve months inside. I was sick of myself, of what I had become as a junkie. I was too proud for this; my ego was too big. I had been born for bigger things.

By then I was nineteen years old, and I had to go inside for nearly two years – not juvie this time, but Norgerhaven, a prison for adults in Veenhuizen. While I was in there, I kicked the coke completely; within those four walls it wasn't on my mind at all.

My parents visited me there from time to time. That time around, my father was very laid-back and sweet to me. "Are you all right, my boy? Are you managing OK in here?"

In Veenhuizen things were much different from what I'd been used to. That was where they held the hardened criminals serving long sentences. These guys were the real deal – liquidations, armed robbery, drug trafficking. They walked around wearing Rolex watches and thick gold chains. "Oh well, just two years inside," they'd say, "and when I get out I have a couple million waiting for me."

Those guys were actually racing mopeds in prison! They even had a swimming pool in the exercise yard, and we were allowed to have our pictures taken to send home to our family. You could get a lot done in here if you had money; there was a brisk trade in all sorts of stuff.

I didn't have a dime on me, but with a bit of fast talk and bravado I managed to get to know people really quickly, and I was soon accepted by the rest. There were also a lot of notorious criminals, guys I had heard lots of stories about, including some people my dad knew. Now I was sitting at their table and eating with them.

Those big guys accepted me. I was one of them. That was where I wanted to belong, to have them accept me. I thought to myself: I'll only go for the serious stuff after this. If I'm going for it anyway, I might as well go deep. That was the life I wanted, and it gave me a taste for more. Finally, I was able to earn the respect I had been looking for all my life – finally to be good enough.

In Veenhuizen I got to sit out the last part of my sentence in an open compound called Fleddervoort. From Monday through Friday I worked in the laundry room that processed the laundry for all the prisons in Veenhuizen. Yeah, that was a real prison environment. I was allowed to go home on the weekends. Just perfect.

When I was out on weekend leave – by that time I had served nearly seventeen of my twenty months – I met a nice girl. Chantal was her name. We had such a good time that I stayed with her for the entire weekend. I wanted my leave to go on forever, but in the end I turned myself back in at Fleddervoort, dragging my feet all the way.

I met up with Chantal the next weekend, and again we had a really great time. I only had to do ten more weeks, but I really didn't want to go back inside again. Even though I knew from experience that it would eventually go wrong, I still wanted to use this time to be outside. It was Christmas, I was in love, and I just didn't feel like leaving her. I planned to turn myself in again after New Year's, but of course it took longer than that. Still, we couldn't go on like that. I was a fugitive. I couldn't apply for welfare benefits, so I didn't have any money at all. For the second time I faced the same dilemma.

My girlfriend was the sensible one. "If we really want to make

BUT THOSE WHO DESIRE TO BE RICH FALL INTO TEMPTATION AND A SNARE, AND INTO MANY FOOLISH AND HARMFUL LUSTS WHICH DROWN MEN IN DESTRUCTION AND PERDITION. FOR THE LOVE OF MONEY IS A ROOT OF ALL KINDS OF EVIL, FOR WHICH SOME HAVE STRAYED FROM THE FAITH IN THEIR GREEDINESS, AND PIERCED THEMSELVES THROUGH WITH MANY SORROWS.

TIMOTHY 6:9-10

this work, you will have to turn yourself in." Unfortunately, she was right.

"When you get out, you can come live with me," she added.
Oh, that would be perfect. Then I could get out of my old neighborhood, away from the place where I had done all sorts of crazy stuff. I would never be one of the big guys there. Once a petty burglar and hustler, always a petty burglar and hustler.

When I moved in with my girlfriend, I would have a chance to make a new start and only do serious business. With that in mind, I decided to turn myself in again after all.

The weather was nice, which didn't make it any easier for me. Reluctantly, I walked to the police station and thought long and hard before I went inside. OK, kid, here you go again, I said to myself. Chin up, shoulders back, chest out, you can do this, don't let them get you down. The doors of the station opened and I walked in.

The officer behind the desk looked at me in surprise: "Can I help you?"

"Yes, I think you can. I still have ten weeks of prison time left, and I'm here to turn myself in."

"Oh, right, take a seat over there." He pointed at a bench. He verified my name and officially detained me. They frisked me and then took me to the back. They put me in a cell without my shoes, and I got to spend the night in a concrete shoebox of a room with a concrete bed and a steel toilet that I couldn't flush myself.

The hum of the ventilation system was all too familiar; it made me feel like I was inside a fridge that never turned off. The concrete in the cell and the vinyl flooring in the hallways gave off a sharp smell that always reminded me of hospitals.

I didn't want to do this anymore. I wanted to be free. Hold on a little longer... As I listened to the keys of the guards jingling, the doors opening and closing, and the hum of the ventilation system, I slowly fell asleep.

The next morning they sent me to Vught, just like the last time. By then Vught had become a penitentiary where they sent everyone who did not come back from leave, or who got into other trouble. The prison had adopted an entirely new regime: every day 23 hours locked behind a door and one hour in the yard. There were no more weekend leaves. It was only ten weeks, but I wanted to be outside, to go to my girlfriend.

I literally just had to sit this one out.

BUT EACH ONE IS
TEMPTED WHEN HE
IS DRAWN AWAY BY
HIS OWN DESIRES
AND ENTICED.

JAMES 1:14

6

LOOKING FOR WORK, FINDING XTC

Finally, my incarceration was over and I could go home. It was awesome to be free, and I enjoyed it to the fullest. We went out a lot and I met some new guys. We would snort coke and really go to town.

Slowly but surely, Chantal started putting pressure on me. She wanted me to wear different clothes, said I had to shave my moustache, and insisted that I needed to get a job. The way I was then apparently wasn't good enough for her either.

I knew from the start that her semi-decadent family didn't like me much, but I thought she loved me just the way I was. When she first got to know me, I was even in prison, so I had thought that she really cared for me, instead of caring about what I did. That turned out not to be the case.

She was an honest girl who worked in clothing retail, which was just fine by me. Her family was all kinds of successful, and she was considered somewhat of a black sheep because she was with me. I didn't really have anything to say when we visited her family, since nothing I could contribute was even remotely connected to their lives.

I was rejected all over again, not just by her family but also by Chantal herself. She didn't even defend me.

When I was falling in love with her, I had been willing to do anything for her, but by that point it was starting to annoy me. That was just who I was; I wasn't willing or able to change. I also had a hard time dealing with employers, so finding a job wasn't easy.

To prove "that I was far better than all those people combined," I decided I was going to try anyway. I got my first job through a temp agency, working in some sort of archive, and I managed to hold on to it for exactly three days. It just wasn't my thing; I couldn't help it. So I stole all the camera equipment I could find and took off again.

For my girl's sake, I gave it one more try, doing my best to find a job. Through an ad in the newspaper, I found myself a job as a door-to-door salesman. My job was to sell art by going door to door: paintings in a passe-partout, a folder filled with all kinds of styles. Supposedly unique, but actually mass-produced on the cheap.

I was supposed to be representing an artists' collective; that was the story I had to spin. These theoretical artists wanted to start a gallery, which was why clients could buy an artwork at cost price. After a nice talk with the owner, I wasn't entirely convinced I should do it. He called me the next day. "I really believe you would be great at this. Think it over again and come join the team."

I didn't know much about art, and I didn't understand exactly how the whole thing worked, but I decided to join them. Together with a group of salesmen, I was dropped off in the middle of some neighborhood. We needed to be back at a certain time. The houses in that area had all been built recently, with plenty of white walls, so selling paintings was going to be a cinch. The paintings sold at two hundred and fifty bucks each, and fifty of those went to the salesman. That was good money!

At the first house, I joined someone else to see how they did it, but I quickly saw that I could do so much better! I did the next few houses on my own, and I was doing so well that I was fifteen minutes late getting back to the van. My boss was angry: "You can't come back late! I'll think you got arrested or something!"

"Man, don't worry, I sold nearly all your paintings." I only had three of the twenty-five paintings left. A whole busload of salesmen were in shock. They had never seen anything like it, especially on someone's first evening!

I had a real knack for it, and easily sold off almost my entire folder every time. I was on a roll.

And then my personality caught up with me again. I wanted to be the boss, not the employee. One time my boss took me with him to the wholesaler where he purchased the paintings. That was nice of him.

Later on, I went back to those guys myself and found out that those framed paintings were sold for fifteen bucks! My boss got two hundred and fifty, and gave us fifty. That meant he was earning a hundred and eighty five per painting. I could do better.

I found someone willing to invest, bought the paintings myself, and told the guys that came to work for me that they could get double: a hundred for every painting they sold. So then I was earning a hundred and thirty five for every painting someone else sold for me: that was a serious raise for my employees and for myself.

We traveled all over the Netherlands, selling tons of paintings and making big money. It was really taking off!

Until I saw a show on TV featuring an exposé about an art dealership. One client said, "I thought I had bought a unique painting, but when I went to the dentist, I saw the exact same painting hanging on the wall! He also told me the same story, about the gallery and the art collective."

After some digging, when it became clear that the exact same paintings had been sold all over the neighborhood, the TV show launched a bigger investigation. They went undercover with my previous employer and showed viewers exactly how it worked: how they added the signature at the bottom of the painting themselves, and how they were supposed to make the sale.

After that show aired, it was impossible to sell any more paintings. After just one year, my business was over and I needed to start looking for something else.

It was time for something better, something bigger. And then something happened to cross my path that really suited me. On one of those nights when we really wanted to party hard, there was no coke to be had. To put it mildly, I was seriously bummed out. I was just in the mood for a good snort!

"Just hold on," said the owner of the place where we were hanging out, "I have something much better for you." He walked to the back and when he came back, he opened his hand right in front of my face. He was holding ten tiny pink pills.

"What are those?" I asked him, still pretty miffed that there was no coke. I had never tried anything but coke – no shrooms, acid, weed, nothing.

But the owner was convinced he had something better for me. "This is XTC. So good! It will really blow your mind."

I still wasn't convinced. "So how much for one of those pills?"

"They're twenty-five each."

My jaw hit the floor. Twenty-five for such an itty-bitty little thing? "Man, that really has to be good!" He had me now.

"Okay, I'll buy one from you, because you say it's good stuff, but if this doesn't deliver, I'll come back here and tear your face off."

The owner didn't seem impressed. "Sure, man, that's fine. I'm not going anywhere, so I'll see you when I see you." He looked at me confidently, so I decided to give it a go and bought a pill. I tossed the pill down and waited tensely. Nothing was happening, nothing at all.

Fifteen minutes later, I got impatient and was all bummed out about the twenty-five bucks I had wasted. I decided to do what I had promised, so I walked over to the owner to confront him.

"Hey buddy, it's not doing anything. And you know what I told you, right?"

The owner looked up in surprise, but he still wasn't impressed. "When did you take it?" When he heard that it was fifteen minutes ago, he said: "Wait, just stand here for a bit." He seemed real sure of himself, so I held my temper and waited a little longer.
Then it hit me.

In the blink of an eye, I felt like I was on fire! It was like champagne bubbling up from deep inside me; my body was boiling and fizzing. The sounds of the people around me faded into a background murmur, and the music completely consumed me. High notes and a pounding beat filled my entire body and transported me to another reality. The feeling was indescribable!

Moving like a zombie, I walked over to the stage. Once I was up there, I took off all of my clothes like it was the most natural thing in the world, and started dancing between all those people, butt-naked. Because I worked out a lot, my body was very buff, so thankfully I did look good. Nobody said anything about it; some ladies even started dancing with me.

For nearly five hours I went completely wild. And I didn't even like dancing! Suddenly the lights went on, and I immediately sobered up. I quickly scooped up my clothes, put them on, and calmly walked outside.

I felt my head in surprise: no pain, no hangover, no nasty taste in my mouth, no nothing! Wow, this was it!

My cravings for coke were immediately replaced by a passion for those little pills. They were great! A new world was opening up for me.

Turned out there were so many types of pills. MDEA makes you mellow, MDA gets you tripping, and MDMA gives you a sense of euphoric love. There were also uppers, speed. I looked into all these different types to figure out how to recognize them by the color and the stamp, and to know which pills were good and which weren't. I soon discovered who to buy them from and who to avoid.

There was an entire business behind the pills, and I was very interested.

7

BRENDA

Things weren't going well at all between me and Chantal. She still kept trying to change me, and that really frustrated me. All sorts of things got thrown across the living room sometimes, from dishes to the Christmas tree.

We were fighting every day, and I got really aggressive, constantly threatening violence. And she'd shout: "If you do that, I'll call the police!" That really made me see red. Furious, I kicked a door in and said, "See, now you have a reason to call the police. Go ahead and call them!" We were often trapped in a downward spiral.

In the middle of all this, she ended up getting pregnant. It wasn't ideal, but I hoped against hope that it would be good for our relationship. Of course we were both happy, too, and it did bring us closer together for a while.

When I held my little boy in my arms nine months later, it felt fantastic. But mainly I was proud to have a son and to be a father; it was a real ego boost.

Sadly, our relationship didn't improve as a result of our child. It was completely unbearable at home; the love was truly over. I started going out with my friends more and more often. We would take pills and stay awake for days.

Meanwhile I was chasing other girls and having affairs. Chantal was no longer important to me.

One night I was completely out of it, high on pills, and I ended up in a sex club that stayed open all night. It was a grim, grungy place with all sorts of shady characters who liked to present themselves as part of the *Penose*, local crime lords. One man was drunk, another was jittery from all the coke, and I was tripping on pills. Just like them, I had completely lost my way. Working girls wearing almost nothing tried to entice the

AND THE LORD SAID:
'IT IS NOT GOOD
THAT MAN SHOULD
BE ALONE; I WILL
MAKE HIM A HELPER
COMPARABLE TO HIM.'

GENESIS 2:18

patrons back to one of the rooms, so they could also earn something off the madness of this world.

I wasn't at all interested in those insistent women. I had been here before, but I had only gone along to a room once, since they would have banned me from coming back if I had refused. "This is a sex club, not a disco," they told me. All right, fine, whatever, but it wasn't my thing.

All male visitors had to hand in their pistols at the door and walk through a metal detector. We would get the weapons back on the way out.

I had two pistols with me that night. When the metal detector beeped, I handed one of them over. I removed the bullets from the clip; I'd get it back again later. After that they thought I was unarmed, but if one of the patrons was looking for a fight, I would be prepared.

It was a seedy room, a couple of slot machines in the corner, the air filled with cigarette smoke. I glanced around me, taking in the situation; who's here, what's the mood like, where am I going to sit? I ended up sitting at the bar, by the corner near the exit. Always on my toes, no matter how stoned I got.

Entranced by the pills I had taken, I let the house music engulf me; I felt like I was floating, like I was someplace else. A cute chick walked in and immediately ducked behind the bar. Short hair, not really my type, but she looked cheerful and chipper.

Abruptly, the stirring strains of the trippy house music were replaced by the rougher tunes of The Cure. The girl behind the bar had switched albums. There went my euphoria; there went my trip.

"Whoa, what was that?! What are you doing? Have you lost your mind?"

"If you don't like it, feel free to go stand outside while you space out," she said cheekily.
OK, irritating, but also funny. Intriguing, this spitfire. Brenda was her name, and I started talking to her.

We unexpectedly ended up deep in conversation, right there at the corner of the bar. No one else was there, just the two of us. But that might just be the way I remember it, because I saw nothing but her at that point. Not that I was falling for her, but there was something drawing us together.

Her relationship was even worse than mine, and she had two children. We were both disappointed, we discovered, both searching for love and for ourselves. We recognized the same emptiness in each other's lives. Saying what we were feeling, we wondered whether you could meet someone and just know: this is forever.

I had never had conversations like this before! And neither had she. It was like being in another world, and I would have been fine going on for hours, even though by then it was very late.

Then a busload of Chinese tourists came in. Brenda immediately got up, saying: "Sorry, I need to go back to work."

There was a brief pause as we looked at each other, and I understood she wasn't talking about pouring them a beer. My heart skipped a beat and my mouth went dry. Shoot! She was a working girl on the payroll here too! I hadn't seen that one coming. I had to choose, right then and there: do I want to let her go, or do I want her all to myself for a bit longer? It didn't feel right to let her go; we had such a strong connection!

Unpremeditated, without even knowing if I had enough money with me, I said, "Oh no, that's not happening. In that case, I'll go to a room with you."

Brenda blinked, but replied resolutely, "No, I'm not going to get a room with you."

"No, don't get me wrong, I won't do anything, but I'll pay what you would get otherwise, and we can keep talking once we're in there."

She untensed her shoulders and her expression relaxed. "You're not work. We're talking; that's a whole different thing."

I definitely agreed with that. I had never thought I'd start anything with one of the girls from the club. I was far too jealous for that. At the same time, I wanted to talk to her, be with her. And I definitely didn't want one of those little tourist guys to go off with her.

I gave Brenda the last of my cash, just enough to spend an hour with her in one of those little rooms. We walked inside and she locked the door behind us. Side by side, we stood there uncomfortably. Eventually, I flopped down onto the bed.

"Relax, just come lie on the bed," I said to her. "I won't touch you, and we can just keep talking where we left off outside." And there we were, lying next to each other for an hour, on the bed where she would normally be working. Nothing happened between us, except talking and getting to know each other better.

It felt very strange, but also very good; we had an inexplicable connection. We were growing closer and closer to each other, mentally in any case. After a while, there was a pause as we both stared off into the distance, and then Brenda suddenly said: "I would never leave my husband for someone else." So she felt it too.

"I'm not asking you to," I reassured her. "You're not even my type."

"Well, I think you're a slick, creepy poser."

Grinning, I poked her side. "But I still like you. I just like you."

After that hour, we left the room and kissed each other goodbye. For just a moment, we gazed deep into each other's eyes. She teared up a bit, and then turned away quickly and walked off. This was really bizarre.

Dazed, I sank down onto a bar stool. It was so weird! Something was happening. I didn't want it to happen at all, and neither did she... But it was happening anyway.

Early the next morning, I got home and ducked into the guest room to avoid Chantal. It was a cowardly move, I know, but I didn't feel like any hassle.

In the meantime, I kept thinking about that cute little bit in the club. She wouldn't leave my thoughts, so I decided to contact her after all. We agreed to meet the next day to have a meal somewhere. It felt like making an appointment with my best buddy, somebody I could be completely myself with, without condemnation.

She laughed herself silly when I drove up in a battered old Mercedes. In her mind I had it all made, but I really didn't have a single cent in the world. My pill business wasn't fully up and running yet; I had just gotten started on it. For Brenda, I had played the grand gentleman who could buy anything he wanted. Now she saw through me.

"I booked a hotel room," I said confidently, hoping that the hotel we were driving to would have a vacancy. I was so eager to impress her!

Fortunately, Brenda was happy to go along with me; of course she already knew where things were heading. The hotel had a room for us, and that was where we slept together for the first time. Deep inside, I knew I didn't want to live without her anymore.

The next time we met up, she had her children with her. Two pretty little blonde girls with sad, sad eyes. They looked neglected, with tangled hair sticking out in all directions.

Of course I had known she had children, but I hadn't expected to meet them so soon. I touched one girl's head briefly; it felt sticky. "What's that on your head?"

Embarrassed, Brenda looked at me. "I just picked them up from my husband's house, their stepfather. All sorts of things went wrong again..."

Every time Brenda went to her work, she knew things would get dramatically out of hand at home. Her children were being systematically terrorized by that man. He talked down to them and emotionally abused them. Brenda had no choice. She was powerless, she said, but it was breaking her heart.

"I can't understand that a man would let his own wife work as a prostitute and treat her children that way," I said to her. I felt so sorry for her and the children. It was no life for them; I could see it in their eyes, and it made me furious! I felt like tossing that jerk off the roof of an apartment building!

We agreed to meet up at her house the next day. I felt more and more drawn to her.

Brenda was drinking very heavily, nearly a liter of vodka-based fig liqueur every day, she told me. That was hard for me. I thought drunk people were horrible; I had been traumatized by my father and his friends. She snorted coke too. Anything to escape the misery.

I understood why, but it upset me. "You shouldn't snort, hon, that's garbage. It's better to take pills," I told her, like I was giving her good advice. "This isn't right, with those kids here. You shouldn't be doing this. At least stop drinking so much."

It was a good thing her husband wasn't home, because I would have eaten him alive! "You know what? You shouldn't stay here; this isn't good for you. You need to get out of here!"

Although Brenda had said she would never leave her husband, she really couldn't live with him anymore either, so she moved out. She was afraid he might give her a hard time, but I made sure that wouldn't happen.

I threatened him over the phone: "You're going to put Brenda's stuff outside and stay really, really far away from her, or I'll kill you." That afternoon her belongings were neatly stacked outside and we were able to pick them up without any trouble.

A week later, Brenda and I were living together in a small room provided by a woman I knew, a friend of mine. My relationship with Chantal had been over before I met Brenda. Although I had just had a child with her, I didn't want to go on being with her; I couldn't.

Johan and Brenda

Things were so different with Brenda. With her I could be completely myself, unrestrained and free. We were cut from the same cloth. We could talk for hours; I could spend the whole night just lying with her on the couch and listening to music.

As far as she was concerned, nothing was required, everything was permitted, and we had great fun together. She made me feel I was good the way I was, and didn't reject me. She truly believed in me; no matter what I said or did, she let me make my own choices.

Her daughters were able to spend time with us now and then, but the room wasn't really suitable. It was small, and not a great place for children. We had nothing to offer them. I was completely unable to cope with the situation; I had just become a father myself, and wasn't really up for parenting someone else's children.

We had no idea where to go from there. Emptiness is what had brought us together, and we kept each other warm. That was wonderful, and I really got along well with her.

But still, at some level I wasn't ready to stay with her for the rest of my life. For the sake of the children and for ourselves, we decided to split up again.

Obviously, Brenda couldn't go back home again, so she moved in with a woman that she was friends with. I went and stayed in the guest room in my ex's house. We weren't in a relationship anymore, but she let me stay there until I found someplace else to live.

Maybe she was still hoping that we would work things out, but my love for her was truly, completely over. It was hell for me to live there, but I soon managed to find a new place.

In the meantime, I kept going out in the evenings, and quickly got involved with another girl. Always on the prowl...

But I couldn't get Brenda out of my mind. She went on vacation with the friend she was staying with, and we talked on the phone on a regular basis. Sure, we also argued over the phone; that was less fun. But I still kept calling her over and over.

I spent hours phoning the reception desk of the hotel she was staying at, trying to get her on the line. Her voice, her laugh, something in her drew me in. Brenda was different. Brenda was more important than I was; I would have done anything for Brenda.

When she got back from vacation, I picked her up from the airport. We hugged each other and I felt more than just friendship for her. Even so, I told her I would rather just stay friends.

"Well, then we should stop seeing each other, because I'm not going to bother with that," she replied. That wasn't what I wanted at all. I was actually completely head-over-heels crazy about her, but I wasn't ready to admit it to myself yet.

We decided to spend the evening together, and we soon got entangled in passionate lovemaking again. It was clear to both of us: we wouldn't be separated again, no matter what happened. So we started spending more and more time together.

I broke up with the girlfriend I had met right after Brenda left, because my heart belonged with Brenda. We had only known each other for a few weeks, but I felt like we had already spent our whole lives together. It was clear: Brenda and I were made to be together.

One evening we were sitting in a dance club together and I sat there gazing at her. Her face had become so precious to me; she was my very best friend.

I took her hands in mine, melted into her bright blue-green eyes, and said, "You know, Brenda, I believe you're the woman for me, for the rest of my life. It's like I've already known you all my life, and I just can't get enough of you."

Brenda looked at me intensely, and it was clear that she felt exactly the same way. "Yes, we were made for each other."

No one around me saw any future in our relationship. My father was also fiercely against it. "What are you doing together? This isn't going to go well! You'll destroy each other." It didn't make any difference. The louder they shouted, the more we were driven into each other's arms.

Of course I understood what they were saying, but I still chose to be with her. What we had together could not be explained, but I knew we belonged together.

At the same time, I wasn't ready to give up my free and easy life yet, so I came up with my own rules for us. "You're my partner. We're together, but if I want to sleep with another girl, I should be allowed to. I want to be able to do whatever I feel like."

I also struggled with the work she was doing. My ego and pride were at stake here: my girlfriend should never have to sell herself to anyone, not for all the money in the world. And really, I also still wanted to live and cut loose as much as I could; I had spent far too much time trapped in all sorts of things. She needed to know where she stood with me; I wanted to be honest about that.

On the other hand, I wanted to keep Brenda all to myself. I was egotistical enough that it sounded very logical to me. Brenda seemed to accept it, although I could sense that I wasn't being entirely fair.

When Brenda said that she hated her work and didn't want to keep doing it anymore, I decided enough was enough: I wasn't going to let her do it anymore. No one was going to lay a finger on my girl; we belonged together.

Right away, we moved in together again, spending all day and all night together. Brenda chose to be with me, leaving her children behind with their biological father – better for the children, and better for our lifestyle.

She stopped drinking, for me. Meanwhile, the pills had become a very regular presence in our lives. And that's how I dragged her with me into the world of drug trafficking.

8

GETTING INTO THE PILL BUSINESS

Brenda and I were on the couch and had already taken so many pills that everything was turning a different color. The pills themselves came in all the colors of the rainbow, with the weirdest logos imprinted in them.

Everybody gave me samples to sell. I tried them all out. Sometimes they were complete junk, but other times they would hit me like a truck. Those were the pills I was looking for.

I had hit a strike of those really good pills. Sometimes my teeth would start chattering, which is apparently a symptom of overdosing on MDMA. One moment I'd be having a conversation, and the next I would suddenly have no clue what I had been talking about.

When I closed my eyes, I was in a different world. Entire movies played out in my head and I felt like an alien back on his own planet, trying to process what he had seen on Earth. When I opened my eyes, I could see colored circles of geometric patterns twisting and turning in crystal-clear clarity, and everything behind them seemed to come alive. I could make what I wanted and see what I wanted. For instance, sometimes a hand would come out of the sky holding a piece of fruit, and I would feel just like Adam taking a bite, but I knew it wasn't OK to actually do it.

We tried every kind of pill and LSD, we did all kinds of things, experienced all kinds of things and above all we partied non-stop for nights and nights on end. Now that I was completely in the scene, I decided to set myself up in the pill business, just a bit. Straight away, my first client wanted to buy twenty thousand pills. "Can you handle that?" he asked me.

"Absolutely," I said. "I'll arrange it for you! Give me a chance."

He did, and I asked around, checking in with some guys I bought my pills from. After a long search, I finally got it done and they gave me the pills.

HE WHO LOVES SILVER
WILL NOT BE SATISFIED
WITH SILVER; NOR HE
WHO LOVES ABUNDANCE,
WITH INCREASE. THIS
ALSO IS VANITY.

ECCLESIASTES 5:10

Proudly, I delivered the goods to my client and got my money. My very first pill deal, and a really big one: those twenty thousand pills earned me about twelve thousand bucks. Wow, that was cool!

I made more and more contacts and got more and more clients. I always bought large quantities which I resold, five thousand to twenty thousand pills. Never ten or twenty. The real thing, right away.

The first customer became a good friend. I sold him a whole lot of pills. During one of our transactions he said to me, "I could see you making the pills yourself."

Surprised, I laughed at him. "Man, I've been working this scene for such a short time, only a couple of months. Don't be silly."

But he still insisted. "You are so driven! I'm sure you could do it." Chuckling, I took his word for it. Maybe, who knows?

Through all kinds of contacts, I was finally getting closer to the source, the one who made the pills. I could order anything I wanted from him; he was able to make anything. The business was really nice, and it went fast; now I didn't need the middlemen anymore.

The batches got bigger and bigger because I was able to offer more competitive prices. Others wanted to earn a profit of one or two bucks a pill, but that ate into their sales.

My strategy was smarter: I was satisfied earning 25 cents a pill, which made it easier to sell – and a hundred thousand quarters was still a lot of money. By keeping my profit margins low, I managed to sell large batches. So much money just made me hungrier for more.

By that point, the orders ranged from ten thousand to a hundred thousand pills, and it was starting to pay off big-time. So we bought flashy cars, fancy jewelry and other expensive stuff, and we traveled to faraway places.

I had also started using cocaine again. Brenda and I used pretty much all day long, snorting ten to fifteen grams a day. My nose was completely swollen and raw from all the pure coke I was shoveling into it. There was nothing we wouldn't do; we were completely into it.

During one of our vacations we flew to the Caribbean island of Aruba. Since we were using a lot of coke at that point, I also took about ten grams with me on the plane. So there I was in the toilet of a Boeing 747, snorting coke. How crazy was that?!

Since the plane was nearly empty, we asked the pilot if we could take a look in the cockpit. I saw a hundred thousand blinking lights, that's how stoned I was.

"That doesn't seem that hard. It looks real pretty, though," I said to the pilot, completely spaced out on the coke. I had a hard time interpreting his look.

We had a layover at Bonaire and I thought we were going to have to get off the plane, but I was still carrying quite a lot of coke. I didn't want them to find it! I didn't want to throw it away, so I just snorted the rest of it in one go.

Of course that made me high as a kite, and I could barely even speak normally. My heart was racing a thousand beats a minute and my jaw was clenched so tight, it felt glued shut.

I had an aggressive stare that said: "I'll eat you alive if you even say one thing to me." My feet were shooting out in different directions because of the muscle spasms; I looked like a guy with a disability. If they had arrested me like that, I'd have been locked up in an asylum right away.

Brenda was freaking out by then, looking at me like I was crazy. How would we ever fix this? Then it turned out that we didn't have to leave the plane at all and could just stay in our seats. Brenda was laughing so hard!

Once we arrived at Aruba, that last adventure meant I had run out of coke. No problem, we quickly discovered, because it turned out that we could score coke pretty easily there, and at ridiculously cheap prices!

I immediately bought a key, my first kilo. It only cost me a couple thousand dollars. In the Netherlands, that would set you back fifty thousand guilders easy. This would hold us over for a while; clean crystals scrubbed white as bone, pure pleasure!

While we were there, my mom and dad were on a cruise, which I had given them as a present, and their final destination was also Aruba. I picked them up in a limousine, like a real Kingpin. That was how I showed them I had seriously made it. I so desperately wanted them to be proud of me. To consider me good enough.

Of course they knew that I was using and how I had gotten my hands on so much money; there was no use denying it. My father certainly didn't approve and tried to talk to me about it.

I tried to argue, "Dad, I haven't been using for a couple of days," but he wasn't buying it.

"Just look at the state you're in! The coke has completely addled your brains." Again the disapproval, but he didn't bring it up again. Perhaps he was just trying to keep the peace, there on Aruba.

I was hoping to get his respect by making tons of money, but that didn't happen. He kept on harping about the things I was doing wrong. My mother would still accept money from me, but my dad wouldn't. The fact that he had even agreed to go on a cruise was a miracle in itself, and sadly it didn't earn me his respect.

We had the time of our lives there on Aruba. I also made an awful lot of money gambling. I played no holds barred and for high stakes, because I didn't care whether I'd win or lose. That was probably why I kept on winning. When I entered the casino, they immediately lowered the prices for the gambling limits at the tables.

Just before we were due to leave for home, I still had a couple hundred grams of coke left. I said to Brenda, "You can say whatever you want, but I am not about to throw that away. This is going home with Daddy!"

So I just brought it along with me in my suitcase. Once I arrived in the Netherlands, I walked right through customs. That was easy as sin; smuggling wasn't hard at all.

My pill business was booming, but then my source started feeling the heat. Law enforcement was closing in on him and he needed to stop. That was annoying, since I already had a couple of big orders lined up. How was I going to sort that out?

My source suggested a solution. "What if I give you my machine and stamps and other stuff, and you start making the pills yourself? When things are calmed down a bit later, we can always see what we do then."

That was exactly what my first client had once told me: I should start making my own pills! The idea immediately clicked in my mind and I decided I was going to do it. But I did have to arrange a location.

As always, I was able to find some guy who was willing to help me. He fixed me up with a hall in an industrial zone. We set everything up in that building: the machine, the mixers and everything else we needed. It was time to get started.

My source introduced me to someone who could show

me how it worked. I was amazed at how simple it was. After just one demonstration, I could already do it myself, almost with my eyes closed. Soon I was also able to arrange the MDMA powder, purchase all the things I needed, and start making the XTC pills all by myself. I was convinced it was going to be awesome.

Just when I thought this was going to be my big breakthrough and I was about to make serious money, things started to go seriously wrong. We had been partying for a while and had gone on a trip. I was still totally out of it when Brenda and I went to the industrial zone together to start manufacturing some pills.

When we got to the building, I realized that I had forgotten my keys. That was a bummer, since we had just driven an hour and a half to get there. I wasn't going to drive us back and forth again.

I soon came up with a simple solution. Using the back of my car, I just rammed the door open. I drove the car inside and started preparing. Not a care in the world.

Well, not a care ... it was still illegal, obviously. So I said to Brenda, "Why don't you go sit at the entrance, and if you see any people, you need to tell me."

I had been busy for a while in the hall when she suddenly yelled back to me anxiously, "Johan, there are a lot of cops driving by."

I had not been counting on that. "What? Are you kidding me?'

"No, Jo, there really are a lot of cops driving around here. Oh, they are all stopping here, eight or nine cars!"

Okay, that meant it was serious. Impulsively, I said, "Come on, let's get into the car and just drive through the shutter door and take off." Yes, I had completely lost it.

Brenda was more sensible. "We are most certainly not going to do that!"

Okay, plan B. "Brenda, you say nothing. Just keep your mouth shut, you don't know anything. I'll just say that I broke into this place. "Excellent idea, right? After all, I did knock out the door?"

Brenda looked displeased, and we decided to go out to them first and try to play innocent. "What's going on? This building is ours, we rent it for ourselves, but I forgot my key. You can call the main tenant and check it out."

The officers seemed nice enough; I was thinking that this might end just fine. At first glance, it wasn't really clear what we were doing there, so we might still be able to get away with it, pretending to be a nice proper boy and girl. Although I was high as a kite on the coke... But hey, it might work.

One of them called the landlord and asked him, "Do you know a Mr. Toet?" Quite clearly, I heard the guy on the other side say, "No, I don't know him."

Wait, what?! What was he trying to pull now?! How hard would it be to just say that I was allowed to be there? Wouldn't cost him one bit and then I could just go home. What a complete loser! Impossible to understand that the police didn't think it was odd that I knew his number, even though he claimed not to know me. But anyway.

They turned me around and put me in handcuffs. Meanwhile, they explored the building and found the hall with the machines, the pills and a weapon. Now I was busted, all thanks to my landlord. I wasn't going to let this happen!

I retracted my previous statement. "Okay, the building isn't mine. I knew there was an XTC plant in there. I confess, I wanted to steal those pills. It's not my plant, it's his. I know him and I know he's in the pill business." All right then! If he was going to claim he didn't know me, he could expect payback.

Brenda and I were arrested for breaking and entering and we were both incarcerated, separate from each other. After almost three weeks, Brenda was allowed to go home, because they finally believed me that she didn't know anything.

"She's my girl and she was just coming along with me," I told them. "She had no idea where we were going."

Based on my statement, they also arrested the landlord when he reported the break-in at the police station. Now it was his turn to throw me a curveball: he named people I was allegedly working with. Armed with that list of names, the fuzz came back to me again. "Supposedly these people are also involved in this, and he is telling a completely different story than you are."

This was heading in the wrong direction and I was starting to feel the squeeze. I didn't want to involve those other people at all! In the end, there was nothing left for me to do but to retract my statement again and confess that it was my plant. I kept my lips sealed about everything else, so I was placed under severe restrictions and wasn't allowed to have contact with anyone. How was I going get out of there?

Then suddenly the odds turned in my favor. The DA had made

an error, so my case was suspended immediately. The error also forced them to release the landlord.

I would still have to appear in court at a later point in time when they subpoenaed me. And just like that, I was out again. Police detectives tried to contact me a couple of times, or so my lawyer said, but I didn't respond to anything; I disappeared off their radar.

They should have never let me go, but I didn't go back.

9

A STUPID ROBBERY

Since I had nothing left but the shirt on my back, Brenda and me moved in with my father-in-law. Everything had gone sour, and if they found me, I would probably still have to face a couple years of jail time. The market for pills was ominously quiet. Frustrated, I tried to think of ways to get money fast.

Even then, we kept going the way we had before, partying and taking drugs, more and more, deeper and deeper, and less and less money. A couple of times, I committed a minor robbery to get some money. Bold as brass, I just walked in somewhere and took the money I found there, without using violence – just heading straight for my goal. People were so startled that they could only watch me take it, without saying or doing anything. I was in and out within 30 seconds.

Sadly, all that money vanished quickly, spent on coke and parties. I felt ashamed of the things I was doing, because it wasn't really me anymore, but my thirst for money was so strong that I just kept going. There was no one to help me get ahead in life, so I felt like I had to do it myself. I really didn't want to get involved in all that small-scale stuff, but I just needed the money!

Our situation was getting more and more desperate. To tell the truth, I didn't see any way out. One day, the two of us were driving along in the car; we had even brought our dog along. No idea where to go or what we should do. No money, a pressing need for drugs, and no future. I was really out of ideas.

Just at that moment we were passing a gas station. As if compelled, I stopped and jumped out of the car. "I'll be right back, Brenda." I pulled my hood up over my head, ran inside and snapped at the cashier: "Empty your drawer, right now! I want all of your cash."

Shaking like a leaf, the boy handed me a stack of bills and I went straight out again. We tore away in the car, but to my surprise I

A PRUDENT MAN FORESEES EVIL AND HIDES HIMSELF, BUT THE SIMPLE PASS ON AND ARE PUNISHED.

PROVERBS 22:3

saw that we were being chased. For a second, I managed to stay ahead of them, but then I accidentally drove into a dead-end street. In blind panic, I slammed my foot on the gas, knocking down all the mailboxes along the road.

The street ended in pastures and ditches; there really wasn't anywhere for us to go from there. It was also impossible to drive back, since there were a couple of cars behind us, and we could hear police sirens getting closer. We were doomed!

Without a second thought, the two of us and the dog jumped into the muddy, water-filled ditch. Completely covered in sludge, we tried to hide in the field.

No, I wasn't going back to jail; I had just gotten out a couple of weeks ago. I hated myself and I hated everything that was happening all over again. The wind blew through our hair as we looked at each other in mild panic, peeking through the reeds. I tried to light a wet cigarette, but I couldn't get it to catch. I just didn't know what to do anymore.

My dog was chasing the sheep; he thought we were just out for a walk. If only I could be as carefree as that dog, completely oblivious. I apologized to Brenda a hundred times for the situation we were in again.

I had fifteen LSD trips stashed in my leather wallet. They were still good. "Brenda, I'm not going to throw these away. We're about to get caught. I'm sorry, honey, I just don't know what to say. You don't know anything, okay? We will see what happens."

The arrest team crossed the wide ditch in a dinghy and entered the field wearing bulletproof vests, their weapons out. Helicopters were flying over us. It almost seemed like being in a movie. But a really bad movie.

I was so bummed out about this. Not that long ago, I had been a serious player in the illegal drug trade, making tons of money, and now I was getting busted for robbing a gas station. Seriously...

I was so confused and desperate, I saw no other way out. "Okay, down the hatch!"

"No!" Brenda screamed, but I put those fifteen LSD trips right in my mouth, all in one go. Immediately after that, we surrendered. Handcuffed and manhandled, we were taken to the police station. They gave us paper coveralls to wear, because the sludge from the ditch had left a horrible stench on us.

It wasn't until we were at the station that the fifteen LSD trips started to work. And boy, did they ever! Once I was in my cell, the LSD kicked in, and it was like I was completely melting into a puddle. My organs, my entire body, the walls of my cell, everything fused together – or at least that was how it felt. Far removed from reality, the only thing I could do was scream at the top of my lungs: "Brenda!! Brenda!!"

Later on, they said that I had been yelling for hours, but I didn't hear anything myself, except for terrible reverbs and echoes, impossible to describe! I wasn't there, but I also didn't have a clue where I actually was. It felt like I was dying; it felt like hell!

A bright ray of light entered my cell from the hallway through the hatch in my cell door; I could almost touch it. When I saw someone standing in front of my open hatch, I thought he was the key to getting me into the light and bringing me to my girlfriend.

I lunged towards him. Without even thinking, I grabbed his tie through the small opening of the hatch and pulled him close to me, screaming over and over: "I need to talk to my girlfriend! I need to talk to my girlfriend!"

Cops came to his rescue and started beating my hand with truncheons, but I didn't feel a thing and just wouldn't let go. The man – who later turned out to be the DA – had his face pressed up against the hatch, fear in his eyes, while I stared at him like a psychopath, screaming at him. In the end, they managed to overpower me and I had to let go. After that, everything went black.

When I came around again, I didn't know where I was or what had happened. They had to transfer me to another station, they told me, because they were unable to reach me; I was completely out of it. I had just spent almost 24 hours sleeping in an observation cell.

Slowly it all came back to me. The gas station, the pasture, the LSD trips ... As soon as they saw that I was back in the land of the living, they transferred me back to the police station. When I got there, I told them I had taken an entire strip of LSD not long before the robbery. That explained a lot.

Immediately, they started interrogating me about the robbery. "Hey man, what happened? It all looked pretty professional. You pull your hood up, you walk in, get your money, walk outside and you're out of there. That was well-planned, except you didn't count on being chased."

"Look, man, I'm not some stick-up guy, this was entirely unplanned. My girlfriend didn't even know what I was about to do. I told her I would be right back. She thought I was going to get cigarettes, but

I had no idea what I was doing, because I had taken that LSD and had been using all sorts of stuff. I've just been really stupid."

"Yeah, that's all well and good, but you caused quite a bit of damage." Well, there was nothing I could do to change that.

Brenda was soon allowed to go home, because I had made it clear to them that she didn't know anything. Pulled it off again. But I was going to have to go to jail.

Suddenly I started to get scared. I realized that I still had that unresolved XTC case! The case hadn't gone to court yet, but by the time I had finished prison time for this robbery and for possession of illegal firearms, that other case would probably have gone to trial. That would be a stretch of years that I wasn't looking forward to at all.

In my cell, I was getting pretty depressed because of my situation, and also because I was still coming down from the LSD. I was back in prison, with nothing to my name, and nowhere for us to go. I was 22 years old. Still hadn't accomplished anything, no future ahead of me.

I felt like a failure, totally worthless, exhausted to the bone and broken to pieces. Brenda was living with her father again, but I didn't even have the money to call her. It was really hopeless. And when you're in prison with nothing, you're also seen as nothing. I couldn't let that happen. It would be horrible if people thought, "No big deal, he robbed a gas station..." That was so beneath me!

I was terribly ashamed to be arrested for something as stupid as a gas station. How much can you get there, a couple hundred bucks?

My shame ran so deep that I called Brenda collect and said, "I am really at the end of my rope here. I'm out. If I don't call you tomorrow, you'll know that I managed to kill myself. I'm sorry, but I really don't know how to go on." Brenda just stayed silent, listening to my depressive rant. What could she possibly say?

When it got dark in my cell again, and life weighed heavy on my heart, I took a razor blade and started cutting into my wrist. I didn't know exactly how I was supposed to do it, and suddenly it all felt horrible. The cut was bleeding, but the blood wasn't gushing out.

I realized that I didn't really want to die. I just wanted to get out of here! I was completely desperate and helpless, because I had totally lost control of my future. But I didn't want to die. I couldn't put Brenda through that, either!

I abandoned plan A and continued with plan B. I mixed the blood from my wrist with water and smeared it all over the floor and walls.

The entire cell was now covered with blood; it looked gruesome. I was also completely covered in blood. By that time, it was midnight and everything was silent. I pressed the button on the intercom of my cell and cried out hoarsely: "I'm dying! I'm dying!"

There was an immediate commotion and guards rushed into my cell. "Oh, God!" they cried out. They pulled me out of my cell, quickly bandaged me up, and then rolled me to an ambulance on a stretcher.

There they discovered that I only had a small cut on my wrist. Just to be sure, they still transported me to the hospital. I had been hoping for that. Once they put me in a hospital room, I would be able to jump out of a window and escape. Then I would be free!

That was a miscalculation. They attached me to the bed with handcuffs! Impossible to open them, so I had no way out. I even tried to rip off the side of the bed, but I couldn't manage to get away.

As soon as they stitched up the cut, they sent me right back to prison. The attempt was a failure. Even worse, they put me in solitary confinement.

I told the warden and the psychiatrist, "I really didn't want to kill myself, I don't know why I did it, it was stupid of me. I just really don't want to be here. I want to get out of here." After that, they transferred me to the Bijlmer prison, just south of Amsterdam.

Because I had told them that I'd rather go to a drug rehab clinic than to prison, they sent me to a ward for drug users. Based on Article 49, I could then spend part of my sentence in a rehab clinic. I rarely used in prison, so I didn't have to go through withdrawal, but everything was better than doing jail time. It gave me some options again and a prospect of freedom. I could already picture it in my mind.

When I had Brenda on the phone one day, I said to her, "When I get out of here, we will have a son. As soon as I can, I will get back into the pill business and I'll make millions again. Nothing will stop me getting there. All of this will happen. I am sure of it."

I had a steadfast belief in it, I was completely convinced that I would succeed. But first I needed to make it through this. I was now completely surrounded by junkies. Not that they were less than me as a person, but that wasn't who I was at all. I didn't beg for drugs, I wasn't down on my knees on the street looking for a few grains of dope. I felt too good for this; I just wanted to get out of there as fast as possible.

I quickly tried to arrange an intake interview at the rehab clinic. That meant a day of leave, going to the clinic accompanied by two guards. My idea was: I would just head-butt the guard in the face, tear myself away from him and then take off. I didn't care if I was cuffed – as long as I wasn't attached to him, I would escape. I was still as quick as lightning; as soon as I saw an opportunity, I'd be out of there. Another new attempt to get out. It gave me hope and I felt positive.

Alas, they sabotaged me again. The prison was reluctant to let me go: "We don't know him very well, he has only been in here for a couple of days, so we do not want to escort him just yet."

I wasn't going to let that happen. I appealed and had the suspension brought before the court: "Your Honor, they don't want to escort me to the rehab center, but my drug use has been a recurring theme in my life. If you don't want me back in here, I need to start doing something about my drug use, because that's the reason I keep on doing these things."

The judge was a reasonable man and said in a friendly tone, "Well, Mr. Toet, you should be mature enough to go by yourself. You'll get a suspended sentence for one day, then you can come back again."

"Of course," I said cheerfully. So I was allowed to leave the next day at eight! The prison disagreed strongly, and they were right. The cell door swung open. Carrying my stuff under my arm and wearing a giant grin on my face, I walked out.

"See you never again," I said to the guards who escorted me to the exit. Brenda was already waiting by the door. I got into the car with her and I was gone. I had absolutely no intention of reporting back to that miserable prison, not a chance.

That was a turning point, I could feel it. Inside that prison, stripped of my ego, I was nothing. I never wanted to go through that ever again. My addiction was the master of me, and that made me do things I never wanted to do, and become a person I didn't want to be.

When I had a lot of money, addiction wasn't a problem for me. Now I was going to do something that was more me. This time I was going to make it big.

THE DEVIL WALKS ABOUT
LIKE A ROARING LION,
SEEKING WHOM HE MAY
DEVOUR.

1 PETER 5:8

10

A FRESH START

My new life started then and there, free and sitting in the car beside Brenda. From then on, things would be different. It wasn't my imagination, it just felt so real. That was how it would be. And it was. Shortly after I got out, I told Brenda after we had sex that she was pregnant. Two weeks later, the test confirmed what I had said.

Six weeks after I got out, I had a pill-making machine again, and was making my first pills somewhere in a back room. In no time, I was back into the pill business and business was booming. Within less than two months, I had gone from zero to hero again, and I felt that it was my moment.

I sold so much product that I could hardly keep up by myself. Everyone had realized that I made really good pills. I was a perfectionist in all aspects of the process; I only wanted the best of the best, so people would be completely spaced out if they took half a pill.

The MDMA had to achieve at least a certain standard of purity, or I wouldn't buy it. The pill had to be a nice color and a specific thickness, and have a specific tablet breaking force. The mark had to be stamped crisply into the pill and be glossy. The pills had to be packaged in dust-free bags, so my customers got a clean, neatly presented product when they bought a bag.

No, I didn't sell low-end crap – I sold quality. And people noticed; I quickly made a name for myself in that small world.

Our baby boy was born healthy, such a special little guy. I felt proud as a peacock all over again. This kid would play an important role in our lives. He felt like a gift from God.

Even so, I wasn't all caught up in the joy of having a newborn this time around either. Because of the way we lived, I rarely saw my other son at all, and now this little guy had showed up too. We really weren't even remotely capable of playing mommy and daddy, although we really did try. The world just had too strong a pull on us to let all of that go. Luckily, my mother helped out now and then, taking care of the little one.

Money and power were what drove me. Plus, I was a wanted man living on borrowed time. I did my best to live life to the very fullest, because it could all be over the next day.

In the meantime, I was incredibly busy running my pill business. I successfully expanded my business, and money flowed into my pockets. Before I knew it, I was driving the latest model Mercedes and all decked out with the most expensive jewelry. I was doing great!

Out of the blue, some so-called buddy of mine asked me to teach him how to base; he said he wanted to know what it was like. I didn't think it was a good plan, since I knew what it had done to me. He brushed my concerns aside. "Oh, come on, just show me how. I really, really want to try it with my girl," he pleaded. Day after day, he asked me, and time and again I explained that that crap really wasn't okay, and that I wasn't gonna touch it again. And still he persisted.

Eventually, I gave up and explained everything so they could do it themselves. It was so weird: they just couldn't seem to manage to inhale the smoke. In frustration, I gave up and demonstrated how to do it. Just one drag, and I was sold all over again. I knew it. And they knew it too... They had set me up, tricked me into trying it. Betrayed, that's how I felt, all over again.

Brenda was my best friend and saw it all happening. But she couldn't keep me from getting bitter and greedy, wanting to be in supreme control of it all. Other people just messed things up for me.

We kept more and more to ourselves, living in hotels and doing our own thing, no one around us. Most of the people who wanted something from me, I just sent away. But sometimes I caught the scent of a good deal and gave it a chance.

That evening was no exception. As the wind howled outside and the rain lashed the windows of my hotel suite, I stared into the eyes of someone who was trying to sell himself to me as a chemist. "Really, if you can invest a million bucks in everything we need, I can make MDMA for you the way it used to be done, and you can earn millions. I would just need a little bit for every kilo I make for you."

AGAIN THE DEVIL TOOK HIM... AND SHOWED HIM ALL THE KINGDOMS OF THE WORLD... AND SAID TO HIM; ALL THESE THINGS I WILL GIVE YOU IF YOU FALL DOWN AND WORSHIP ME.

MATTHEW 4:8-9

Should I buy into it this time? Despite all my disappointments, I was inclined to give it a try. I once said: "Tell me what I need to do to be rich, and I'll do it." I would have done anything for that. I had no limits.

Why didn't I have any fear of the risks I was taking and the people I was doing business with? Was it because by that point I no longer cared about anything, and that living or dying were equally fine with me? In any case, there I was staring at someone with an icy glare who said he was willing to work for me and make millions for me. I had a little over a million there. That would mean that I had to go all-in, with all the dangers it might entail.

Oh well, nothing ventured, nothing gained! I walked to the safe. I gave him fifty thousand bucks, just handed over the cash right there. "Here's something for your trouble, and I'll contact you this week."

After a quick market survey, I discovered that I could make the MDMA, the main ingredient for a pill, for less than a quarter of the current market price. That meant I could not just make the very best pills, but also the very cheapest. I also discovered that many of the pill dealers would love to purchase MDMA to make their own pills. That sounded promising, so I went for it.

That did mean that I would have to employ some people to help me do a lot of the work. That was how I met Chubbs. I had an instant click with him. Almost immediately, I confided in him and let him make a lot of money, because I felt he deserved it.

Why did I keep on doing that? Apparently, I had learned nothing from my previous experiences, when I trusted my so-called friends and they inevitably all betrayed me. Was I hoping against hope that I would finally meet a real friend? Who knows... Brenda warned me, but I didn't listen. This time I was going to make it, I was sure of that. It was my decision.

Chubbs became my right-hand man and helped out in all sorts of ways. He transported the pills and the MDMA powder, and he collected the money from the people who purchased my product.

I was mainly in charge of production. By that point I had invested over a million guilders and bought large tableting machines so I could produce more pills per hour. For the chemical process, I bought all the chemicals I needed to make powder from the oil, and all the equipment that went with it. I started out with two hundred liters of oil. After the entire process of synthesizing and crystalizing, the entire batch was ready three days later.

The floor seemed almost covered in flakes of white gold, pure MDMA glittering in the bright light of the heat lamps. It was the purest you can get, two hundred and forty kilos of MDMA, enough to make over two million pills. The entire hall smelled sweet and I felt the euphoria of victory coming over me. There was an absolute fortune lying here, and all of that in just three days! I had it made!

For weeks I kept working non-stop. My chemist quit because he couldn't handle the pressure. That wasn't a problem for me: I snorted myself into oblivion to keep from falling asleep, and made hundreds of kilos of MDMA and millions of pills. The money was pouring in. I could buy what I wanted and do what I wanted. Still, it was never enough and it didn't make me happy. What was wrong here?

THEN I LOOKED ON ALL THE WORKS THAT MY HANDS HAD DONE... AND INDEED ALL WAS VANITY AND GRASPING FOR THE WIND. THERE WAS NO PROFIT UNDER THE SUN.

ECCLESIASTES 2:11

11

LOST IT

Brenda had been spending a lot of time in Portugal. We had been there a couple of times before and had bought a house there. So I was sometimes alone for days on end. During those times, I was manufacturing continuously, day and night. It was all about making pills, snorting coke and then cashing in. The sound of the machines was like a voice saying: mo' money, mo' money. I loved that voice.

The next order of one million pills had already come in. I could barely handle the work. Fortunately, I had a couple of friends to help me: my best friend cocaine to keep me awake, and my good friend machine gun to reassure me.

I had just manufactured a hundred and twenty kilos of MDMA. I was still hazy from all the chemical waste products that had been stacked against the walls like a ticking time bomb. If the police walked in on me like this, then I'd be in real trouble. In my madness, I resolved to shoot a barrel to pieces. Boom. No more evidence. Probably also no more Johan, but that didn't really sink in.

The ocean of white MDMA was once again spread all over the factory hall. The fumes of acetone rose up from it, permeating all the pores of the building, and mine too. It smelled like an elephant's nails were being polished! I felt euphoric: I saw a fortune in white powder that had been oil not all that long ago, and soon it would bring me a lot of money in the form of a shipment of pills. A fascinating process, I simply couldn't get enough.

The customer for the one million pills asked if I could hurry up the first batch because he had to move it fast. I gave him my word, even though I'd have to really bend over backwards to make it happen. By that time, I had been working so many days and nights in a row that it all blurred together into a manic spiral. At the end of the day, I had the first batch ready for delivery, but my drivers were all busy taking care of stuff for other customers.

Because I had given my word and it was a pretty good client, I decided against all of my principles to deliver it myself. I threw a huge barrel filled with 250,000 XTC pills into the trunk of my car. My hair, eyebrows, nose, my clothes, my shoes; everything was covered in white powder. I looked like I had just walked through a huge pile of plaster. I smelled sweet, had a dopey look on my face and felt like a zombie. I quickly took a good snort of cocaine, grabbed my pistol, locked up the place, and got into my car. Time to take a ride, get a bit of fresh air.

In the car, I stared intently, wired from the coke and wired from the tension because my eyes kept closing from fatigue. To keep my eyes open, I started to talk out loud to myself, hit myself in the face and scream like a psycho. Every time I nodded off for a second, my head jerked up and I was awake again. It was a madman's ride.

Finally I decided to pull over onto the shoulder of the road, because I couldn't go on any longer. I stopped my car and it was lights out for me. I dreamed I was sleeping on a bed at the beach.

Suddenly I heard pounding from far away, and voices. "Sir! Hello! Sir!" Would you stop, I was thinking, what lunatic was trying to wake me now? I ignored the sounds, but they kept on getting louder. "SIR! ARE YOU ALL RIGHT!? CAN YOU PLEASE OPEN UP!" I heard a couple of times in a row. Still the loud pounding. "OPEN UP, NOW!"

When I finally managed to open my eyes, I could see that I was not at the beach at all, but in my car! Police officers had surrounded my car and were yelling at me. Oh no! As best as I could, I tried to pull myself together. Suddenly I remembered the pills in the trunk, the gun tucked in my waistband, the coke in my coat pocket, the fact that I was a wanted man and didn't look all that great. How was I going to get out of this...?

I thought quickly. Then I opened my door and put on a sad face. A cop said, "Good day sir, what are we doing here? Are you all right?"

"Officer," I said, half-sobbing. "You know, I am so stressed out. I work in a bakery and my boss is on a two-week holiday. For ten days now, I have been getting up at three in the morning to bake bread and not getting to go to bed until late at night. I'm just on my way home from work and I am completely exhausted!"

I swiped the crocodile's tears from my face with my hand. "I think I must have fallen asleep. I am so, so sorry, officer. I didn't even have the time to dust myself off."

The cops looked at me, dumbfounded. They had not expected to hear that story. It had to have been the truth, since I was white as snow. They looked at me closely once more, conferred with each other, and then sent me back on the road with some advice: "Sir, we will let you off with a warning this time, but you need to go straight home and get some rest. This can never happen again. You need to take better care of yourself!"

"Oh thank you, officer, I absolutely will. I will drive straight to my destination, you can count on that. Thank you for your understanding." I got into the car and couldn't help but laugh under my breath. Relieved, I delivered the goods to my customer, got my money and then took off again. The shenanigans were done for the day. I took a break for the night and ended up in a way-too-expensive hotel room, somewhere in the center of a city. I had no clue where I was.

Night had fallen and the world outside my hotel room was coming back to life. I heard police cars coming and going, people screaming, drunk ramblings and girls giggling. The street lanterns in the street, the brake lights of cars, they all flashed through my window. I had the feeling that I wasn't part of it, that I wasn't from this planet. I lit a cigarette and counted my money.

Two hundred and fifty thousand guilders, not bad for an afternoon's work. I just put it with the rest of the money, on the big pile. It actually had no value for me anymore, but for a moment it slaked my insatiable hunger. I had just had a narrow escape. Now it was my turn; I was going to enjoy my success.

I boiled a sizable bag of cocaine, turning it into big cubes of about five grams each. The game was on. How long would I last before I got paranoid, started having weird ideas and started checking the gap under the door to see if anyone was coming to arrest me, rip me off or liquidate me?

I prepared a base bottle and put the coke on it. Then I took my lighter. One last time checking the room. Everything was locked up, my weapon was in my waistband, cocked and ready, the other gun was ready for action under my pillow, the music was off, the TV was off. Everything was ready.

I emptied my lungs completely, placed my lips on the pen and lit the lighter, holding it over the coke in the bottle. Then I took a deep breath until the entire bottle as well as my lungs were completely filled with the white smoke from the cocaine, which popped and crackled and melted and burned in the bottle. The adrenaline raced through my body, I was still holding in the smoke in my lungs. I put the pipe down and then exhaled. The entire room filled with white smoke. Within a second it felt like I had left my body. The feeling of euphoria was more intense than the hottest sex you can imagine. I felt like a god and wanted to stay like this forever.

It only took a few seconds for me to start hearing voices whispering in my head and seeing shadows around me. Fear washed over me so intensely that I grabbed my gun and looked around skittishly. The euphoria turned into a nightmare. Feverishly, I cleaned up all the drugs, got rid of the bottle, and hid the money, the jewelry and the weapons. Any minute now, it felt like the police would come busting in, or others who wanted to rip me off or harm me. There were demons swirling around in my head and they were driving me insane. Where should I go? What should I do?

Again I grabbed my gun and peeked out from behind the curtains. I was high as a kite, completely wired. I placed my ear against the walls of my hotel room and tried to listen closely, then crawled like an assassin on my stomach across the hallway carpet to the front door and positioned my head so I could peek through the gap under the door to see if anyone was there. My heart was pounding in my throat: I could see shadowy outlines, but I wasn't sure whether they were shadows conjured up by the cocaine or if there were actually people in front of my door. I lay waiting behind the door, not moving a single muscle.

Ugly thoughts raced through my mind faster than the speed of sound, my finger on the trigger, sweat dripping down my face. My jaws were clenched and I needed to make a conscious effort not to grind my teeth. My feet were moving in all directions; I was twitching uncontrollably. My eyes were opened so wide that I could feel a headache gnawing in the back of my head, but I tried to keep my focus on the gap under the door.

The clock was ticking, and you could have cut the silence and tension with a knife. And then... The flash of the coke slowly dissipated, my body began to relax and I got up from the floor. As always, it had been a false alarm. I went ahead and snorted a few lines of coke for good measure and took a sip of water, toked the next pipe, and rode the next nightmare like a rollercoaster, again and again.

This dance of madness continued on through the night, and for many nights after. Every time dawn broke, I wondered a thousand times: how long can I keep this up?

O, WRETHCHED MAN
THAT I AM!
WHO WILL DELIVER ME
FROM THIS BODY OF DEATH?

ROMANS 7:24

12

I'M OUT

Chubbs was my right-hand man, and by then I trusted him implicitly, giving him complete freedom to decide what to do. I shouldn't have done that.

At some point he had been off the radar for a couple of days, so I decided to drop by his house. There was someone home, but Chubbs wasn't there. I decided to go inside and see if I could find any clues of where he might be.

And then I suddenly found huge piles of my own pills and stuff that shouldn't have been there – pills that we had supposedly lost. The sneaky bastard had been stealing from me! What a filthy cockroach! Deceiving me like that, when I would literally have done anything for him, and had given him everything he ever asked for. I treated him like a brother, and he just ripped me off behind my back! I was in a hellish fury!

Chubbs must have figured out that I was on to him and that we were through, because I never heard from him again. I found out that he and his girl were living somewhere else and that he had started working with my competitors. Treason to the highest degree.

Once again, I had trusted someone I shouldn't have. Everyone I had been loyal to, everyone I wished the best for and would do anything for, had double-crossed me, betrayed me and robbed me. How could that happen to me every time? And why did I always find someone else to trust after that?

Of course I wasn't a sweet, innocent boy myself, but to the people I chose to call my friends I was one hundred percent fair. Those 'friends' apparently saw things differently.

That had been the case from when I was a little kid. My heart was broken time and time again: by my father, by my schools, by my so-called friends. Over and over, I was rejected. I gave it my all and put up with it all and swallowed it all. In return, I wanted them to be loyal to me

BUT THE COMPANION OF FOOLS WILL BE DESTROYED.

PROVERBS 13:20

too. I wanted them to think I was good enough. Such a tough guy, yet so insecure. It was rejection. Pure rejection.

That was the last time, I decided. From now on I would only use others to get ahead, just like they had used me for their own benefit: eat or be eaten. I would never trust anyone ever again, ever; I was sure of that. Brenda was the only one I could trust; she was the only one who always had my back, who was always with me and had faith in me. She would never betray me or deliberately hurt me; she would never abandon me. I trusted her, and no one else.

I was so tired and fed up with everything and everyone. The hate and malice bred by all that betrayal. I just wanted to leave it all behind. No money in the world could ever soften that blow.

I just wanted one thing: to get out and move far, far away. The law was also hot on my heels; since I still had over six years[1] of jail time to serve, it seemed like a good time to leave.

Brenda moved to Portugal ahead of me. I sent my stuff there as well, and took two weeks with Brenda to find some peace and quiet together. During those two weeks, I didn't use anything at all. Being clean helped me find myself again and think clearly for once.

I needed to go back one more time to settle some things in the Netherlands: sell off my inventory, get money from everyone who still owed me, and then get myself out of the country.

Once I got back to my factory in the Netherlands, I again bumped into all those people who wanted to profit from me. Like hungry wolves, they were staring at me and drooling with greed.

Now that I was clean and sober, I could see what a bunch of losers they were! They were rats and all they wanted was to rob me blind. They betrayed me blatantly, pinched my pills and told me that a customer hadn't paid when they actually had. They did business using my name and then messed it up, putting the blame on me, which made me some enemies I didn't deserve. I didn't even bother denying it, but I threatened them as viciously as they threatened me.

My so-called best buddies thought I wasn't on to them. I wasn't going to say anything yet, or they might still try to pull crazy stunts. First I made sure I got everything to safety. Only after that would they realize I had pulled the plug on the whole operation. What a shock that would be!

I wasn't going to be able to pull it off and still stay clean. We were talking about an awful lot of money here. I needed to adopt a certain attitude, like none of it actually mattered. "Hey man, do you have the money ready? I'll drop off new stuff for you tomorrow." Then that customer would think to himself: "Oh, I'm going to be restocked." But he wouldn't.

But I was really going to need some coke to put on a convincing act. I was so close to telling them the truth, and I needed to avoid that at any cost. I had to take back what was mine; once that was done and dusted, I would tell them the truth... but by then my money would be safe.

Brenda came to the Netherlands with me and was in the hotel. "Brenda, I'm sorry, but I'm going to need coke if I'm going to finish this my way. Otherwise it won't work." Brenda wasn't happy about it, to say the least. But I still did it.

Once I had retrieved all my money and moved it to Portugal, I planned to pull the plug and sell the factory. I didn't care one bit how people would react; I was completely fed up with everybody.

13

LONELY IN PORTUGAL

There I was in Portugal, together with Brenda. Our son was often with a babysitter, since we were mostly freebasing and completely out of it. Brenda's daughters were still living with their father, and my other son was living with his mother. We could do whatever we wanted.

I had needed the coke to wrap everything up, but now that it was over, I found I couldn't bring myself to quit again. After all the betrayal and deceit, the sense of loneliness kept me trapped in the drugs, and I didn't know how to break free. I had tried to quit so many times already. Sometimes I had managed to do it for as long as a few months or half a year, sometimes only a few weeks. Usually it fell apart when I had accomplished something and thought to myself: I've earned a reward... and then used again. Coke had been a recurring theme in my life for fifteen years – and now again.

It was a delight, and also an escape. Coke was my very worst enemy, but also the love of my life. Coke gave me a sense of direction, even though what I experienced was often like hell. Sometimes I would literally see demons crawling out of my walls: black, oozing creatures. Sometimes I was completely swarmed by rats, or voodoo stakes with skulls would spring up from the ground. I didn't have any connection to faith, but it felt like I was in hell.

Everything was dark and bleak, negative and terrifying. A continuous stream of voices whispered lies into my ears that everyone was out to kill me, get me, that I couldn't trust anyone and that everyone was hell-bent on doing evil. 'They' were coming for me, and I never knew who 'they' were. I plugged my ears with chewing gum so I wouldn't be able to hear the voices anymore. But they weren't coming from the outside, they were in my head! The war was being waged inside me. I saw terrible things; horrendous words washed through my mind like a dark flood.

And yet I was still drawn to coke. The aggression and madness

In front of the villa in Portugal

on the one hand, and on the other that sense of vulnerability, the feeling of being safe and secure, feeling connected to the cocaine because it numbed everything. I was willing to suffer the madness, because I wanted that other feeling just as much.

Besides Brenda, there was nothing and no one else in my life. I couldn't be with my family, not the way I was on drugs. Cocaine came first for me. My madness, my world, that was what it was all about, and I found it harder and harder to hide it.

At times like that I would lock myself up in the bathroom, since I really didn't want our son to see me that way. When Brenda took him to the babysitter for a couple of days, we would spend all day and all night snorting coke again, losing ourselves in complete madness.

When our son was three years old, Brenda decided to stop using. From then on, she was less and less OK with me doing coke for such a long time, day after day. She decided to rent an apartment where she could retreat with the little one when things were too much for her to deal with.

She knew that I was her husband and that we belonged together. She was so good for me and would never leave me. She was devoted to me, my angel who rescued me, my one true friend in this world. I wanted to be with her, but the drugs had me in their clutches.

Sometimes I just sat at home all alone, smoking coke. There was nothing else for me to do. I had tons of money, so I bought all sorts of things that I really didn't need. I wasn't even enjoying it. When I saw a nice big yacht, I'd say, "Oh sure, gimme one of those." A Ferrari? Sure, I'll take that, go ahead. Another house. I never went there; I didn't even use the things I bought. I drove that Ferrari maybe five times, sailed the yacht twice. I had no one to share it with.

Once in a blue moon, my family would come down to visit, and then we would take the boat out for a spin. That was about as much as I could handle, one single day. I couldn't handle more than that, because I was a complete coke-head.

I had a camera system installed on top of my house that let me observe things up to a hundred yards away. The system cost me a fortune. All night I would sit behind those color screens and zoom in. Who was that person I saw there? What was that? My house was protected so well it almost seemed like Fort Knox; it was impossible to even get to my gate without being seen. My coke was delivered over the fence while I stayed inside, voluntarily locked inside my fortress. Completely lost, at the lowest

Under the influence of drugs

THE THIEF DOES NOT COME EXCEPT TO STEAL, AND TO KILL, AND TO DESTROY.

JOHN 10:10

point in my life. Walking to the toilet was too much effort for me, so I started peeing in a bottle. At the bottom of the bottle I could see a layer of white flakes. There was so much cocaine in my urine that it crystallized.

I started locking myself up in my bathroom more and more often. Completely wired on cocaine, I would sit there and talk to myself, an unstoppable stream of words. Nothing left but deep, gloomy darkness and ego-tripping.

When I looked in the mirror, I was terrified by my horrific reflection. I could hardly recognize myself, almost demonic. My eyes were huge, round and pitch-black, my grimace malicious and bleak. What kind of life was this?

Sometimes I would put a cocked pistol against my head, longing to pull the trigger because I hated myself. "I can't stand this anymore; I'm going to shoot myself in the head!" I would yell at the phantom in the mirror. I was almost completely oblivious to the fact that a mother was watching her son die from coke, that a woman was seeing her beloved husband sink deep into madness, that my children didn't have their father, that there was so much pain, sorrow and worry in the people who truly cared about me.

I didn't realize that they needed me too. It was all about me; I wallowed in my self-created misery. I was skin over bones and completely beside myself, totally consumed by evil. Because I was hardly eating anything, I was frequently light-headed, and the drugs only made it worse.

I observed things I normally couldn't have seen. I had opened the spiritual gates of darkness and let everything in. I had surrendered completely.

Things couldn't go on like that. A long time ago I had said, "Once I turn 30, I will stop using." Back then that seemed like a long time. But now, after my thirtieth birthday, I had run out of excuses and yet I was still using. Just me, on my own.

I had walked around a couple of times with a statuette of Jesus in my hands. Somehow I had always found such things beautiful. A cross, some statues of saints; I didn't understand any of it, but they did have an effect on me. The way that many people have a Buddha figure in their homes because they believe it gives them peace. How bizarre, a figurine made by human hands.

But anyway, I had Jesus as a statuette, my good friend when I had lost my way. I had whole conversations with that statuette.

The statuette of Jesus

"Well, Jesus, here we are, just the two of us." I made jokes and talked to it like it was the most normal thing in the world. In reality, I was completely crazy.

Nearly two years had passed since I started living in Portugal. I could have lived a good, normal life here with my little family, and been really happy. But my reality was the exact opposite. Disappointed, rejected and broken, I was locked up inside my own prosperity. My heart was totally black; there was no light and no hope.

It was the end of August 2001. I hated myself. This life was totally pointless. Worthless, that was how I felt: worthless and dirty. I wouldn't even have wished this on my worst enemy. I might just as well be dead. Despair was taking hold of me. From the very core of my being, I suddenly started to cry. Something inside me knew I could only expect help from above.

Torn by inner pain, I screamed with all of my being: "God, if you truly exist, you need to help me, because I am going to die. I will not survive this, help me! Oh, God, if you exist, then help me. I am dying, I don't want to live like this anymore. Help me... I just can't get out of this anymore. Here I am, help me."

And I kept screaming like that, pushing it out of my lungs, my arms stretched wide. With the last of my strength, I called out, a deep cry of distress to heaven, to God, but nothing happened. Nothing at all.

See? Even God was just a figment of people's imaginations. Everything was fake, everything in life was empty and false. I had been disappointed yet again. All my hope was gone... and yet I kept living.

Nothing had changed; my life was still a dull, empty state of misery. Day in and day out, I stuffed myself to the gills on coke, without any hope or prospect of a future. Lonely and broken.

Then it was Christmas Eve 2001. By that point Brenda had been sober for quite a long time, and I really admired her for that. She spent a lot of time in her apartment. Once in a while, she dropped by to bring me food, but she quickly left again because I was too far gone.

That evening I was alone. No family festivities for me; I was completely spaced out. I was surrounded by all sorts of glasses with foil and some coke, a lighter and cigarettes. There I was, completely off the rails and looking for ways to numb the pain of my loneliness. I picked up my base glass and tried to take a hit. Oddly, for no apparent reason the glass slipped out of my hands and broke on the floor.

Cursing under my breath, I prepared a new glass. Again, just as I was about to inhale, the second glass fell to the hard floor and shattered into a thousand shards. The next glass also fell. And the one after that.

What the hell was wrong with me? Couldn't I even hold a glass? It almost seemed like they were being knocked out of my hand every time. I really didn't get it! I eventually ran out of glasses. Unbelievable!

And it wasn't just the glasses that broke. My lighter stopped working, and my coke kept falling on the ground. No matter how much I wanted to smoke the coke, on foil or any other way, I just couldn't get it into my body! It was so annoying!

In the end, I called my dealer to order new stuff. He was always there within five minutes, because I was his best customer. Every week he would bring me one hundred, two hundred grams. He picked up the phone, and I said to him in my limited Portuguese, *"Amigo, cem gramas, rapido!"* "Friend, a hundred grams, quickly!" His answer was short and to the point, the usual way we communicated: *"Cinco minutos."* Five minutes.

Five minutes later and he still wasn't there, and an hour later he still hadn't arrived. That was odd; he always came immediately when I called. When I called him to ask when he would get there, he said again, *"Cinco minutos."* But again he didn't come.

Restless and agitated, I tried to scrape some of the coke from the broken glass on the floor, but it was useless. I smoked one cigarette after the other. My entire body and mind were craving another high, a new flash of coke, so I could get back on that high-speed train of madness and escape the hellish reality I was living in. So I kept on calling, but nothing happened.

Around four in the morning, I was all done trying. It almost seemed like I had been cursed; I apparently wasn't allowed to have the coke! Frustrated, I put down my phone and gave up. For the first time in weeks I went to bed voluntarily without any coke. Not collapsing into an exhausted coma, but just going to bed to sleep. Defeated, I lay down on my bed and fell into a deep sleep.

When I woke up, I immediately checked my phone. My dealer still hadn't returned my calls. But I realized I didn't really care. Funny enough, I actually felt very good, refreshed. Something had changed inside me. A thought suddenly popped up: this is the time, quit now.

I immediately called Brenda and asked her, "Could you pick me

BEING CONFIDENT OF THIS VERY THING, THAT HE WHO HAS BEGUN A GOOD WORK IN YOU WILL COMPLETE IT.

PHILIPPIANS 1:6

up? I just quit." Brenda wasn't convinced at first. "Well, you might want to see if you are still so sure about that this afternoon."

"Yes, but I just quit. It's okay, I'm done."

"Okay, fine, but just to be on the safe side, call me back in the afternoon."

After that phone call I walked into the living room. I could clearly see the devastation I had caused in my high-priced villa. I had wrecked all my expensive furniture, and the glass top of my coffee table was shattered. Everywhere I saw holes in the doors, places I had punched through in fits of anger. The house was covered in glass and cigarette butts, paper and random junk, empty bottles, bottles filled with urine. Everything was musty, gray and stale. Three huge piles of laundry nearly reached the ceiling. I hadn't done laundry in ages; I just kept buying new clothes. It was a huge mess.

I walked around astonished, thinking: how did I get here? Who did this?! It was like the fog had lifted. I just wanted one thing and that was to get out of that devastation, out of that house!

In the afternoon, Brenda picked me up and took me to her apartment. She looked beautiful, like an angel. And there was another angel, my youngest son; he was magnificent! Suddenly I could see them again as they really were: so beautiful, people who loved me, so extraordinary!

Totally exhausted, I lay down on the bed and immediately fell into a deep sleep. I surfaced for a few moments, and then fell back asleep. When I woke up again, I saw that Brenda had made me something delicious to eat. She was so sweet. After a few bites of food I fell back asleep again.

I spent Christmas Day and the day after that drifting in and out of sleep. After three days I was somewhat rested and had even gained a couple of pounds. I still didn't feel any cravings for coke – but honestly, that had happened before, but I had still started using again after a while. I did understand why Brenda still didn't trust the situation.

But I was convinced: it is over and done. I had gone clean and was free of my addiction. It was bizarre how I had managed to do it, and I was hugely proud of myself that I kept going, even though I couldn't explain how.

It was wonderful to be home again and spend some time together doing fun things. On New Year's Eve the two of us went out to a

THEREFORE LET HIM
WHO THINKS HE
STANDS TAKE HEED
LEST HE FALL.

1 CORINTHIANS 10:12

big party. There were some guys there who had been supplying me with coke all that time. One of them walked up to me: "Man, I just got the best coke from Colombia, just look at this! All crystals, the best coke you can find! Come on, let's go to the bathroom and have a snort."

I looked at him calmly and said, "Is it really that good?"

"Yeah, man!"

"Okay, then use it all yourself. And the next time you offer me some, I'll break your nose."

The guy gaped at me. "What?!" That couldn't be right; I never said no to coke. Too baffled to say anything else, he walked away.

I immediately felt the temptation to start using again. It was still my vulnerability. But I wasn't falling for it again this time. Brenda realized that I really had changed. "This is the first time that you turned down coke. Now I really am starting to believe you quit! I'm so proud of you!"

Of course I struggled every now and then, especially in my mind: come on, you've been clean for so long, you could have just a little bit... It's such nice weather, you have something to celebrate. Those kinds of stupid lies. But I saw through the trap and stayed clean.

In movies I would see dudes who had scored a big haul and would go off and snort a line or two. Yes, that made me want to scratch the itch too. Oh right, that's what it was like. There was no real danger anymore, but it still remained a sensitive issue. Every day I had to make the choice again: "Not today, today I am also clean. Today I am clean."

But I couldn't get rid of all the traces in myself just by snapping my fingers. No matter how clean my house was, every day I could still feel the damage in my heart and head. Still, I was doing better every day and I could even smile a bit more often.

After a month or two of clean living, I was headed in the right direction; I was sure of it. Miraculous. For fifteen years I had put coke into my body almost constantly, until my body was only fed by coke, and still I felt really healthy today. It felt like an entirely new beginning – although I still didn't know where my life should be heading.

WHOEVER REWARDS EVIL FOR GOOD, EVIL WILL NOT DEPART FROM HIS HOUSE.

PROVERBS 17:13

14

THE LAST TIME

Just when I had quit everything and was ready to live a clean life, my uncle came to visit. "Can you help me to make pills in the Netherlands?" he asked me. "We can get our hands on a machine and MDMA, but we don't know anyone who can make these things. Could you help me with that?"

Again, temptation beckoned. I didn't want it, but it drew me in. For him, too, I wanted to do my best to get money and power, to gain status. For him, I had always wanted to be good enough, even back when I was just a little boy. I looked up to him. And I still wanted to prove that I could do all of that, and make him rich in no time. Then I would finally get the recognition that I longed for.

In spite of that I told him, "Sure, I'm willing to do that for you, but I won't go back to the Netherlands. Can't you get everything here instead?"

He had everything transported to where I was, and I started making pills in Portugal, in a villa owned by an acquaintance. It wasn't really a big factory and it was just a small machine, but I still managed to manufacture a hundred thousand pills in one day. Everyone involved caught the tempting scent of money: it was so easy, and the payoff was so big.

I sold my first batch of pills to a Spaniard, even as I was cleaning up my act and buying a new house. I wasn't interested in that business at all anymore. It was a repetition of the void, and I had long ago stopped experiencing the sense of excitement. Honestly, my heart wasn't in it anymore; I was starting to hate it. As far as I was concerned, we would stop as soon as we had sold this batch.

Then I ran into a snag. Our Spanish customer suddenly backed out of the sale. He was in trouble and wanted to get out of the business for a while. So now who were we going to sell these hundred thousand pills to? I didn't have any contacts in Portugal to sell the pills to, and I wasn't going to go around marketing them randomly. I had cut ties with my whole network in the Netherlands. How was I going to get rid of them?

The first person who showed an interest, I gave a thousand or five thousand pills to sell. It still wasn't moving fast enough for me; those small-scale batches weren't getting me anywhere. After it was over, I wanted to set up a small business and live a quiet life, and leave this all behind me. I started looking even harder for people who might want to buy the pills.

A while ago, a buddy I had met in Portugal had introduced me to someone who had been interested in doing business with me. But he felt a bit off to me, so I had decided to keep him at arm's length. Then one day I ran into him at the gas station. He said, "Let's meet somewhere, because I really want to buy some product off you." Well, all right then; I did need to get rid of those pills. "You know what, I can give you five thousand pills." I was thinking, if he rips me off, which was a legitimate fear, it would 'only' be five thousand pills, but if he wants to do real business, I would be able to get rid of those pills.

My mother and my youngest son were in the house we had bought for my parents. I still had eighty thousand pills stashed in that house. I agreed to meet with the guy in a park nearby.

Together with Brenda, I was waiting in our BMW. A bit later, he got into the car, along with a buddy of his. "Just drive, we're going to pick up the money," he ordered.

"We didn't bring anything with us," I said to him, but he reassured us that it wasn't a problem. Fine, I wasn't worried, because they couldn't do anything to us if we weren't carrying anything. A bit later they had me stop the car, but they didn't get out; they stayed sitting in the back seat. Something was off, I could feel it. I was intensely sorry I had ever suggested anything to the guy. I should have just flushed those pills down the toilet, then I wouldn't have had any more hassle.

Suddenly someone grabbed me from behind and pulled me into the back seat. The tip of a big knife poked menacingly into my side. In broken English, the man said, "Stay calm, or else I push it in." Furiously, I struggled to free myself, but it didn't have any effect. Then the other guy got out of the car and pointed a shotgun at Brenda, saying "You need to get in the trunk."

"No one goes into the trunk!" I cried out immediately. I started kicking and cursing again, attempting to wrestle myself free. Who did they think they were!

Brenda also put up a fight. "I won't get in the trunk!" she screamed.

The man with the shotgun reconsidered, saying to her: "You stay in your seat and shut up." He got into the car next to Brenda, making her take the wheel, and pointed the shotgun at her to keep her under control.

Meanwhile, the guy next to me was digging that knife even deeper into my side. "We want it all: your jewelry, your money, your car, everything. If you don't give it to me, I will kill you both." Then another guy got in, and a girl who could speak better English, and we started driving again. We were at their mercy; they had that knife in my side, the shotgun pointed at Brenda, and who knows what other weapons. We had been kidnapped!

If only I had brought my pistol along, this would have been a blood bath; I would have blown all their heads off. I was absolutely furious, and also seriously offended! What the hell could I still do now?! Speaking Dutch, I shouted to Brenda, "Pull on the wheel and cause an accident, or we aren't going to survive this!" Immediately, she jerked the wheel hard and the car swerved back and forth across the road.

Unfortunately, the kidnapper was very alert and quickly corrected the car's course. Right away, he gestured toward Brenda like he was going to hit her. "Don't!" I yelled. I needed to keep a cool head now. Brenda was my most precious darling, and I didn't want her to get hurt.

"Listen, what I have is far more than what you're asking for. Here, take my Rolex, my bracelet, you can have it all. The car isn't even registered in my name, so it's no use to you. I don't have any cash money. But we do have a box of pills back at home. I can give you that, and it's worth at least two hundred and fifty thousand euros."

"Okay, fine, we'll take those pills." Over there, you can sell pills for anywhere between three and five euros each. Of course they were interested.

So they drove to the park and we walked together to the house. Meanwhile, they kept a gun pointed at Brenda. "One wrong move and we'll shoot her," they threatened. Tensely, I walked in front of them, thinking: my mother is in that house, with our child.

The ripper walked beside me, along with another dude. If only I had stashed a gun with my pills. I always used to do that. There was no way out now, no matter how hard I tried to find it. What would keep them from killing us all once they got their hands on the pills? We had been kidnapped; God only knew what else they might be capable of.

Back in the Netherlands, they would never have dared to pull this on me. But nobody knew me in Portugal; they just saw me as a solitary foreigner who was dealing drugs and had a ton of money.

When I walked into the house, I saw my mother standing there. Her face changed immediately; I could see that she knew it was a bad situation.

"Hey, mom, nothing's wrong, they just want the pills. Everything should be fine." I said to the guy, "Don't hurt my mom. Look, here's the boxes, everything is in there."

Thankfully, we quickly left again. We walked back to the road and they pushed us back into the car. Somewhere between our house and the turn-off, they got out of our car and into another car. "We'll throw the keys somewhere over there." Then they drove off.

As soon as I could, I ran out of the car to get those keys. I dove back into my BMW and chased after them. "I'll push them off the road! I'll just make them crash; I'll force them off!" Brenda tugged on my arm and yelled: "Let them go; deal with that later!" I realized: Yes, police... all those pills, the whole situation... and I didn't have a weapon on me either. She was right. Much calmer, I drove home again.

The next day, I did arrange two guns for myself. We were both pretty much in shock, and we definitely didn't want to go through that again. Fine, those pills were out of my hands. Fortunately I was still alive, and no one had been hurt, or worse. Even so, that kidnapping did something to me. It made me even more wary.

Later I heard that the same dude had ripped off some other guy and then got beheaded in retaliation. He had scammed lots and lots of people, so everyone hated him. In the end, that was what killed him.

My uncle was seriously bummed out that we got ripped off, so we decided to make one more batch of a hundred thousand pills and at least get some profit out of the whole situation. I had a hard time selling those pills, too.

I had already disassembled the machine and put it in my own garage, ready for transport to the Netherlands. I was also going to have to stash the pills at my place, because my friend's was up for sale. I felt an even bigger urgency to get rid of everything. All this needed to be kept hidden. After all, I wanted to build a new life.

Meanwhile, the police were still hot on my trail. I heard that people had been mentioning my name in the Netherlands. After we had parted

FOR ALL WHO TAKE THE SWORD WILL PERISH BY THE SWORD.

MATTHEW 26:52

ways, they moved on with their own business. When they were caught, they had apparently decided to place all the blame on me.

The police knew I was in Portugal because some people had betrayed me, and phones had been tapped. The Portuguese were all set to arrest me as soon as the Dutch authorities gave them the green light. They had already staked out my high-security fortress, keeping a close watch to see what I was doing there. But they hadn't moved in on me yet, because I wasn't doing anything. I just sat inside all day, seeing no one and speaking to no one.

I was in their sights now when I went to my boat or went out to see other people. They saw my uncle; they saw the van we used to travel around in. Because I really didn't want to get caught here, I was extra careful. The sentences were long in Portugal, and the prisons were terrible. Just a little longer, and it would be over and done with. I just needed to move these pills, and then I was through doing business in Portugal. Then there wouldn't be anything they could do to me.

15

TOO LATE

Unfortunately, that wasn't how things went. One day they arrested a couple of petty criminals for possession of pills. They told the cops who they bought them from, which led them to the person who got them from me.

Of course that person told the cops he had bought the drugs from me and Brenda. At that point they definitely had enough evidence to arrest me for real. So they came and got me. By that time, they knew exactly what I would be doing and where I would be.

At dusk that evening, I was walking my dog, like I did every night. Like always I said to my little boy, "See the stars? Aren't they beautiful? God made them." Strange... I didn't know God, but I still talked about Him pretty often.

After tucking our son in bed, I went and sat down in front of the house, in the front yard overlooking the road. I was waiting for Brenda, who was picking up money somewhere. This wasn't my usual routine; I normally sat in the garden behind the house, out of sight. It took a really long time for her to come back. As the sun set and night fell, I sat there and looked around me.

I suddenly felt uneasy and was absolutely certain: my life will never be the same again. Something is going to change radically. It was an incredibly intense sensation. No idea what it was, but I was absolutely consumed by worry.

We were going to go look at a new house the next day. We already knew we wanted to have it; we just had to say yes. Was that the total change? It felt different, much more ominous, not positive. I just hoped Brenda would come home quickly. Could something have happened to her?

Her car finally pulled up; she had no idea how anxious I had been. Relieved, I gave her a kiss and we quickly went inside. A new

BECAUSE WHAT MAY BE KNOWN OF GOD IS MANIFEST IN THEM, FOR GOD HAS SHOWN IT TO THEM. FOR SINCE THE CREATION OF THE WORLD HIS INVISIBLE ATTRIBUTES ARE CLEARLY SEEN... SO THAT THEY ARE WITHOUT EXCUSE.

ROMANS 1:19-20

phase of our life would start tomorrow, and we were really looking forward to it!

The new day dawned. The sun rose, and I was up bright and early. I showered and quickly got dressed. Holding my son's hand, I went to let the dog out before we left. Hand in hand, we walked through the grain fields beside our house. The dog raced out in front of us.

As always, no one else was around; the people who lived in this area were all so anonymous. Big villas surrounded by high walls, and cameras everywhere: it was like we all wanted to hide away from the big, bad world outside.

Suddenly, I saw a car turn into a dead-end road. That was odd, so early in the morning. I immediately recalled the kidnapping. It wasn't all that long ago, so I was immediately wary. The car made a U-turn and stopped, and several men got out. My heart started beating faster and I gripped my little boy's hand tightly. No one was going to lay a finger on my child.

They started calling out to me in English. But I was in Portugal, and they were clearly Portuguese. Why would they be speaking English to me? How could they know that I spoke English? This wasn't good. Now what? Was this another kidnapping attempt? I pushed my son behind me. The men walked toward me and pulled out their pistols. 'Policia!'

And then I knew. This was the total change. Crazy, how I had felt it coming the day before. And then I was pulled back out of my thoughts, as two police officers holding their pistols stood right in front of me.

"Señor Toet?"

"Yes," I answered, knowing that it was all over now.

"Hold your hands in front of you." Calmly, they put me in handcuffs. My son and I were put into the back seat of the car.

"It's OK," I said to him. "It's all right." I was glad that it was the police, not another kidnapping. They drove around the block with us, asking all sorts of questions.

"Do you know why we picked you up?"

"I have no idea, but I'm sure you're going to tell me."

"You're under arrest for suspicion of drug trafficking, running a criminal organization, and possession of firearms. You're in big trouble, sir." Yes, I know that. That's obvious, smart guy.

By the time we got back to our house, the streets were full of police cars and vans, sounding their sirens. Inside, Brenda was handcuffed to a chair. So intense! They took me into the house so I could show them where the pills and other stuff were stashed. They treated us respectfully and were very friendly.

"Sorry, sweetie," I said to Brenda, "I'm so sorry about this." If they only arrested me, I would be fine with it. Of course at times I had thought: what if my family and I ended up in some prison in a foreign country? Fear of that possibility had overwhelmed me more than once, but I had always quickly pushed it away.

Now it was becoming a reality. A thousand thoughts raced through my head. What would happen now to our child, our family, our things, the money, our lives?

Meekly, I showed them where all the stuff was, since they were going to find it anyway. For the last time, I looked around at the house. We had just spent twenty thousand euros making it habitable again. The kitchen was pristinely white and neatly tiled, the walls were spotless, the furniture was beautifully clean, and the windows sparkled. I saw the big sliding doors of my house open and looked out into my garden.

Everything looked gorgeous; the wind ruffled softly through the palm trees and the water in my swimming pool sloshed gently against the edges. Such luxury, and I had never really been able to enjoy it. Now I would never come back here again.

I showed them the pill-making machine, and the pills were in plain sight, right there in my shed. I was really done for.

After marveling at our beautiful home for a while, one of the police officers said to me, "You have everything, you live a dream life... Why do you still do this business?" It was almost like they had some sort of respect for me. Maybe because this wasn't just another raid. I grinned, thinking to myself: dream life? You have no idea what you're talking about. You can only see the outside.

I occasionally tried to catch a glimpse of Brenda and my little boy. My son had no idea why Mommy was tied to a chair or why Daddy was in handcuffs, walking through the house with all sorts of men. Ashamed, I looked down at the ground. What kind of man, what kind of father was I...?

By that time, they had also found the weapons, the jewelry, and the cash we had lying around, and loaded it into their van. Then they put Brenda and our little boy into a police car. They took me to a different car. I looked back at our house one last time. Regret, anger and sorrow filled my heart. What a mess, and it could have been so beautiful.

Then I heard the dog barking desperately. "My dog!" I called out, but of course she couldn't go with me. "Let me ask the neighbors to take care of her until someone picks her up for me," I asked them. Thankfully, they agreed to that. My dog was so important to me; they weren't going take that away from me.

When we arrived at the police station, I was taken straight to an ugly, dirty, old jail cell. It smelled terrible and was incredibly filthy. Would they be holding Brenda in a dirty cell like this? No idea where they had taken her, but I wanted to see her!

They laid out all our pills at the police station and had me show them how the machine worked. They calculated how many pills we could make in one hour, so they could work out how many pills I had produced in total. They made a big fuss about it, and I knew: we're in really deep shit.

Brenda was done for too, although she was only peripherally involved. She knew what I was doing and was always with me, but she would never have done this if I hadn't dragged her along with me. She would sometimes pick up the payments or drop off a bag of pills. Even though she only played a minor role, they had seen her doing it, so she was arrested too. We had both been caught red-handed.

It made front-page news: 'XTC lab shut down in Portugal, the first in history!' Everything was exaggerated. I was already clean and wrapping things up. I didn't want this life at all anymore; everything was supposed to be different. Everything was already different! But no one cared about that...

Our little boy was sent to my mother in the Netherlands, and Brenda and I were sent to separate prisons. The drama was now complete. Now I was truly alone, and lonelier than ever. I prepared myself for what was going to happen next. It wasn't going to be any fun, but I would hold my head high and go down like a man, if it came to that.

Police close drug 'factory'

Police have shut down a major drugs "factory" and seized 82,991 ecstasy tablets from a house in Albufeira. The Faro PJ arrested two foreign suspects and four Portuguese nationals aged between 19 and 35 at the factory and seized laboratory equipment.

The factory apparently specialised in producing pink and orange tablets with a ring logo stamped on them, which police suspect were distributed across Europe. According to Gonçalo Amaral, the co-ordinator of the investigation, officers have discovered that the network has links with several other countries and police expect more arrests as their investigations continue.

...hile the GNR ha...

ACASOS

DROGA

'ECSTASY'

Foram descobertas no Algarve 83 mil pastilhas

'Made in Portugal'

Foi descoberta a primeira fábrica portuguesa de 'ecstasy', em Albufeira. Ao fim de um ano de investigações, a Polícia Judiciária apreendeu ali 83 mil pastilhas e outras substâncias utilizadas para fazer a droga, além de três armas de fogo, munições e dinheiro. A PJ deteve ainda dois cidadãos estrangeiros, suspeitos de se dedicarem ao fabrico do produto, e quatro estudantes que o vendiam, todos com idades entre os 19 e os 35 anos.

XTC laboratory in Portugal

POLÍCIA JUDICIÁRIA FAZ MAIOR APREENSÃO

Ecstasy era feito em Albu...

Laboratório produzia milhares de pastilhas por dia

MADALENA BENTES ■ Faro

A Polícia Judiciária (PJ) de Faro desmantelou, em Albufeira, um laboratório de fabrico e comercialização de ecstasy, o primeiro a ser detectado pelas autoridades em território nacional. A operação resultou na maior apreensão deste produto no nosso País, num total de 82.991 comprimidos.

Na sequência da acção, denominada 'Operação Laboratório', foram detidos seis indivíduos, com idades compreendidas entre os 19 e os 35 anos, dois dos quais de nacionalidade estrangeira, responsáveis pela fábrica instalada na região há pelo menos um ano. Os restantes quatro suspeitos, todos portugueses e estudantes, dedicavam-se à revenda do produto no mercado nacional, a partir do Algarve.

De acordo com o coordenador de Investigação Criminal da PJ de Faro, inspector Gonçalo Amaral, a operação resultou de investigações realizadas nos últimos doze meses, período durante o qual foram efectuadas diversas apreensões de comprimidos identificados com o mesmo logotipo, consistência e cor, provenientes do referido laboratório. Trata-se, segundo se apurou, de 'pastilhas' fabricadas com produtos provenientes de um país europeu, não divulgado pela PJ, revestidas das cores salmão e rosa, que apresentam uma das bases o desenho de um anel.

Características que permitiram aos inspectores da PJ localizar o laboratório onde operavam os dois estrangeiros, cuja nacionalidade não foi revelada.

Na residência onde se encontrava instalada a fábrica, protegida por um sofisticado sistema de vigilância electrónico, foram detectados, para além dos comprimidos já acondicionados em várias dezenas de pacotes destinados à revenda, composição de ecstasy e objectos necessários à sua produção, entre os quais, embalagens de corantes e uma prensa. No local foram ainda apreendidas três armas de fogo, um computador, um automóvel e dinheiro presumivelmente proveniente da actividade ilícita.

CIRCUITO INTERNACIONAL
De acordo com o inspector Gonçalo Amaral, o laboratório desmantelado em Albufeira era responsável pela transformação final dos comprimidos de ecstasy, fabricados a partir de produtos que entravam em Portugal através de um circuito internacional, cuja ligação a esta rede está agora a ser investigada.

A 'Operação Laboratório' contou com a colaboração de outros departamentos nacionais da Polícia Judiciária, com vista a apurar a área de actuação da rede, desde o Sul ao Norte do País.

▲ A DROGA ESTAVA ACONDICIONADA EM DEZENAS DE PACOTES

QUATRO MORTES EM PORTUGAL

...Quatro mortes verificadas em Portugal, no ano passado, estarão relacionadas com o ecstasy, de acordo com os exames legais aos cadáveres indicaram, a par de outros estupefacientes, a presença de MDMA, a substância activa desta droga sintética que desidrata e pode aumentar o ritmo cardíaco, bem como, segundo estudos estrangeiros, causar lesões no sistema nervoso central e no fígado.

PRINCIPAIS APREENSÕES

DATA	LOCAL
2002/Maio	Leiria
2001/Março	Samora
2002/Janeiro	Lisboa
2002/Fevereiro	Matosinhos
2001/Maio	Lisboa
2002/Maio	Arrábida
2001/Março	Lisboa
2002/Junho	Estoril
2002/Abril	V. R. S.

*quantidade em milhares

16

IN PRISON

Stone-cold sober, I entered the prison... And what I saw before me was nothing short of hell. The large concrete hall was filled with their threatening presence. Dozens, maybe even hundreds of prisoners, spread out into various smaller groups, but all of them paused and turned to look at me, the new guy, for one long moment.

To the right and left of the large concrete hall I saw two floors of cells, closed off with steel doors. The corners of some doors were bent; I could imagine how that had happened. A couple of the windows were broken, and there were cigarette butts and plastic cups all over the floor. No, this was definitely nothing like a Dutch prison.

And there I stood, holding a blanket and a toothbrush, nothing more. The door fell shut behind me with a loud bang, the echo lingering. Behind that door, I had just been subjected to a thorough search.

Their hands had been everywhere, in places I didn't want them to be. Spread your buttocks, lift your scrotum: nothing was too private. I knew the ritual, but it was still so humiliating. Having them bark harsh commands at me, right in my face, even though I didn't understand a word of Portuguese. And they refused to speak English, no matter what I tried. "Get real, man! What do you want me to do?" It made me feel irritated and rebellious.

I had heard enough about foreign prisons to know I was really in for it now. The charges against me were serious, so I would definitely be here for a long time. Meanwhile, I had lost everything: Brenda was in a prison all the way on the other side of Portugal, my children were far away, and my house and my possessions had been seized by the authorities. Everybody was being watched; there was no one I could call.

And here I was, surrounded by all these men. All of them looking at me, wondering: who is this guy? I knew this game well, so I stared right back at them: bring it on! Bristling like a pit-bull, I was ready to lash out, to survive.

I quickly scanned the hall. That group of aggressive-looking Russians wouldn't do; those guys would pick a fight way too fast. There were lots of young Portuguese kids strutting around and making a lot of noise, but I didn't want to be associated with them.

Somewhere off in a corner, a couple of European-looking men were calmly observing the room. They kept talking among themselves, but they were keeping an eye on me. Those had to be the more serious fellows, more laid-back than those young kids. That's where I needed to be.

I walked toward them confidently. Before I even got there, they started talking. "You're that Dutch guy, aren't you? We saw you on TV, man. You're going down for that XTC factory, right?" My reputation had gone before me. It felt good, even though I was in a horrible predicament.

Right away they wanted to know all about me, and they had littler fish who wanted to arrange things for me: clean my cell, get me coffee, and so on. That's how it worked: the people at the bottom of the ladder work for the people on the rungs above them. Services provided for two cigarettes or a phone card with one euro on it. Convenient.

But first I wanted to figure out who was who, before getting in too deep with anyone. I would be fine on my own; I didn't need anything quite yet.

I had guessed right about the tension between the Russians and the Portuguese. The Russians were bossing everyone around, and the Portuguese soon got sick of it. If that ended up in a turf war, people would get killed; things were pretty intense.

Right from the start, I saw how things worked around here. I figured out that the food was terrible and that there was no schedule. Everybody hung around in the prison yard or outdoors from first thing in the morning until early evening. The guards hardly ventured out among the prisoners, and when they did, it was often in response to an incident, and usually too late.

The cell doors were shut from seven in the evening until the next morning. During those hours, we were at the mercy of our cellmates.

My eight-person cell contained four bunkbeds, a sink and a hole in the ground; that was it. The rest of the people in my cell were Portuguese, and they had their own thing going; I wasn't part of it. Tricky business.

We were packed together tightly; from my bed I could see the

THE LORD YOUR GOD IN YOUR MIDST, THE MIGHTY ONE, WILL SAVE.

ZEPHANIAH 3:17

hole in the ground, and it was incredibly disgusting. The hole was surrounded by splashes, and it was never cleaned.

There were all sorts of noises coming from the other beds that I didn't want to hear. Some of them had sex with each other during the night. I wore earplugs to block it out. I turned to the wall and couldn't stop thinking: my God, where have I ended up? Sleep wasn't even important; I just didn't want that kind of crap so close to me.

I didn't have to fear for my safety, since I soon discovered the Portuguese were no threat to me. That was very reassuring; it's exhausting to feel unsafe everywhere, even in your own bed. I did have to stay alert during the day, though. Anything could happen; someone might just stab you in the stomach because he didn't like the look of your face.

Once I saw ten, fifteen men jump a kid out of the blue. They kept going until their target stopped moving, and then they were out of there, gone before the guards even arrived on the scene. The injured kid was carried away, no idea where to.

"Who did this?" the guards shouted... but they knew as well as we did that they would never find out. No one said anything. If you did, you might be next. I never saw that kid again.

I didn't pick any fights. I just kept my head down and tried not to make any enemies. Danger was lurking around every corner, so I always had to watch out. Sometimes I had difficulties, but then other people stepped in and sorted things out for me. "Leave this man alone, boy, or you'll have a problem."

I didn't want any hassle. I was just trying to survive and mark out my territory. I did that by making friends, partly by using money. That's how it worked.

Luckily I had found a way to get my hands on my money again. That made my life inside much easier. Guards were easy to bribe. Their difficult, dangerous jobs paid less than minimum wage. For a few hundred euros, they'd get me food from a restaurant, bring in groceries and telephones: anything you can imagine and more. I even had watermelons filled with vodka smuggled into the prison, and I didn't even drink alcohol! I just did it for the status.

Money was power. I had known that my whole life. Money bought me everything I wanted. It was always about me, about what was better for me. I never saw the consequences of the money for them. I only cared about achieving my own goals.

I gave a couple cigarettes to a boy who squeezed me a glass of fresh orange juice every morning and cleaned my cell every day. This kid stuck to me like glue. He was crazy as a loon, but loyal to the bone because of those couple of smokes I gave him every day. He could always get his hands on food, but those cigarettes were really precious to him. Man, oh man, a couple of euros meant nothing to me, and he was so grateful!

Only now did I see what money could do for other people. Giving changed me. It wasn't just about me anymore.

One of the boys spent two hours every day waiting in the infirmary to pick up ibuprofen for me. I'd had a chronic headache since I went to prison, possibly because of the tension and the focus I had to maintain all day long in there. I didn't feel like waiting around for those painkillers myself.

He was helping me, but I realized that I was also helping him. I got rid of my headache, and he had a couple of smokes and something to snack on.

Boys would wash my clothes in exchange for food or money. I wouldn't miss it, even if I gave away a thousand euros, but it was worth a lot to them. And they stayed loyal to me. Unlike so many people I used to give so much money to.

More and more, I realized that there were people in the world beyond myself, and that life was precious.

At the same time, I had an emptiness inside me that nothing could fill. That void made me start taking a long, hard look at myself. What a jungle it was, that whole drug scene.

And how amazing it was that I had gotten clean and didn't even crave it anymore, even though I saw people using drugs all day long. Those guys were completely oblivious and could hardly stand on their own two legs.

All at once, that was no longer my normal, even though I had been part of that world for fifteen years and only been off the drugs for six months. Truly incredible!

It was liberating, but at the same time, I was in prison, trapped within the walls of this hellhole. How would I get out?

THE LORD IS NEAR
TO THOSE WHO
HAVE A BROKEN
HEART, AND SAVES
SUCH AS HAVE A
CONTRITE SPIRIT.

PSALM 34:18

17

LOSS AND CONVICTION

My heart was breaking at the thought of what I was missing. Every little thing I remembered was painful to me. His tiny hand felt small and soft. My arm was tugged back slightly; his little legs couldn't quite keep up with me, so I slowed down to match his pace.

Hand in hand, we walked along the vineyards that stretched out in front of our house. Every evening, we went for a walk here: my youngest son, the dog and me. The night had swallowed the light, letting millions of stars shine through in the sky. And that one, it was so beautiful, so bright.

"Look, son," I said. "Do you see that star? Isn't it beautiful? God made it."

I rubbed my hand roughly over my face. It caught me in its grasp: that emptiness, that moment. I had taken it for granted, that walk around the block every evening with my little boy. I had no idea who God was, but I knew: He's there, He exists, and He is powerful. And my youngest son listened. He was with me. Back then, he was with me.

And here I was now, all alone. He was so far away, so unreachable. I couldn't take him for walks anymore, just talk to him on the phone occasionally, but what do you say to a toddler? We no longer did anything together; I was no longer a part of his life, nor the lives of my other son, or Brenda's daughters, who I loved like my own children... I was clean and sober, and being all alone hurt so much...

I saw that star again, and I knew Brenda could see it too at that same moment. From her cell on the other side of Portugal, we were thinking of each other, connected to each other. But I missed her so terribly!

Since I was apparently a high-profile criminal, a flight risk, I wasn't allowed to go visit her, even though others were allowed to see their loved ones. They simply didn't dare to risk transporting me. Ridiculous.

I wasn't allowed to call her or write to her either. My letters were intercepted and combed for clues. I started sending letters to one of Brenda's cellmates, and she sent her letters to another inmate in my prison, who passed the letters on to me. I wrote lots and lots, and all the letters were about love. By that point, I had also arranged a telephone so she could call me secretly, at the same time every day.

Brenda was in a cell with thirty other women; she hated it in there. Her misery made it even more painful to miss her so much. I wanted to be with her, and with our little boy.

I didn't dare to think about my other son and Brenda's two daughters. I had never made time for them, really taken the time to get to know them; I had always been so focused on myself. I never taught them what was right... I failed them so badly.

I wanted to get out of there, out of this worthless life. I could buy anything, but I had nothing. What had all this cost me? What could I still look forward to?

All these guys in here had the same dreams and ambitions as I did, even though most of them hadn't made it so far. The wall of my cell was decorated with photos of my cars, my table covered in jewelry, my villa and all that cash: the so-called proof that I was the real deal.

These guys wanted to be near me. I had status; I had it made. Sure, I was good enough. Wasn't that what I had always wanted? Getting a pat on the back, making an impression, being a winner. Well, mission accomplished. Great job!

Only now could I see that their laughter was fake. Now I realized: this is such a terrible world.

I asked to switch a two-person cell with Julio, one of my cellmates; amazingly, our request was granted. Now we had a place of our own: much better, more peace and quiet. We planned to make the best of a bad situation together.

We became friends, and I promised to help him set up a company when he got out. His plan was to buy up limousines for cheap, get them legalized, and then sell them on for a profit. I would give him the first limo to get started.

Julio wanted me to join the business too. "No, I'm not going to be part of it," I said. "Once I get out, I'm gone, headed back to the Netherlands as fast as possible. I'm all done here!"

Julio taught me Portuguese, mainly using the subtitles on the

FATHERS, DO NOT PROVOKE YOUR CHILDREN, LEST THEY BECOME DISCOURAGED.

COLOSSIANS 3:21

many films we watched together. Obviously that was a great help to me in my contact with the Portuguese prisoners. I was able to find the right people, communicate better and better, and of course unload my frustration about how corrupt it all was. Not how corrupt we were, but how corrupt the system was, how negative its impact was, and how terribly long everything took.

Two years in pre-trial detention before sentencing; that was just ridiculous. Why couldn't it be done in a couple of months? Two years in uncertainty, two years without visitors, no leave, nothing. And no one would appeal, because that took even longer.

Lawyers came and went. They wanted to earn money, and promised me golden results. "Fine," I said to one of them. "I want my house and my stuff back. I want a minor sentence for myself, and my wife needs to be sent home. Let's hear your plan."

With dollar signs dancing in his eyes, the lawyer said, "If you pay me fifty thousand euros, I can make this happen for you." Wow, that was lots of money.

Even though I had the money, I didn't trust his offer. How could he possibly help me? I was pretty sure I was done for: caught red-handed with an XTC factory and eighty thousand pills ready to be sold. What on earth could a lawyer change about that?

"Can you guarantee that you can make arrangements for me?" I asked him. No, he couldn't, so that wasn't going to happen. "I can come up with a better way to spend that 50K."

In the end, I 'only' paid five thousand euros to my lawyer, and she did her best for me.
She found out that seven guys had been arrested with pills that I had allegedly produced.

"I don't know those guys, and I didn't sell anything to them!" I exclaimed when she told me.

"Yes, but the Portuguese don't care about that. They see a link, so they've decided you're leading a criminal organization. The sentences for those crimes are much higher. You could get up to twenty-five years, but obviously we're going to try to reduce that."

Twenty-five years? Get real! What was that even? Twenty-five years: I couldn't even imagine it. But it was real; I knew that a couple of guys had actually gotten twenty-five years for drug trafficking. That's so incredibly long, I wouldn't make it.

My lawyer reassured me: "It probably won't be that long for you." But when I told her how often I had been in prison, how I had fled the Netherlands, and what I had done there in Portugal, she laughed a bit and added, "In that case, twenty-five years really is a possibility! Because you kind of did, well... um... It's not your first time behind bars, now is it?"

I didn't think it was funny at all. "Make it clear to them that I didn't have anything to do with those guys!"

Over and over, I was picked up for questioning, but my answer was always the same: "I have nothing to say."

My uncle was mentioned a couple times, too, because my phone was tapped when I called him, but I denied any knowledge of anything. "Can't I even call my uncle?"

I was very bothered by the fact that Brenda was still in prison too, and I spent a lot of time thinking about how I could get her released.

Finally my trial started. By then it was 2004 and I had been in prison there for two years. It was quite a circus. I was still a high-profile case, obviously, so a group of ninja-style people surrounded me to escort me to the armored car. Motorcycles drove before and behind us, and the route was blocked off like I was a war criminal. I wasn't allowed to take anything with me, and I was handcuffed the whole way there in the car.

First they drove around the courthouse a couple times. There were people everywhere, some holding cameras, and armed men with bulletproof vests and police dogs. Eventually the car came to a stop in between all sorts of other vehicles. The door opened, my head was pushed down roughly, and I was hustled inside, quick as a flash. I wasn't allowed to talk to anyone.

The trial took from nine in the morning until ten in the evening. I was all by myself in court all day long, between that whole row of ninjas, who tensely kept a constant watch over me and the surrounding area.

All the other suspects and Brenda were in a quiet room where they could talk a bit and use the bathroom. When I needed to go to the bathroom, they let me wait forever.

Exhausting, that's what it was. Just tell me the sentence already, get it over with. But apparently it wasn't that simple.

BUT HE WHO DOES
WRONG WILL BE
REPAID FOR WHAT
HE HAS DONE,
AND THERE IS NO
PARTIALITY.

COLOSSIANS 3:25

The first session didn't go very well, and the court filled up all the way again after the break. I didn't know any of the men they had arrested, but having them there made my case so big.

They were bummed out about it too. Being linked to me also made them look like they were part of an organization, which made their cases more serious too.

Brenda was also pulled into it, but she was only involved at all because she was my wife. Things were truly looking bad. We were both in prison and couldn't be with our children. The way things were going, we were going to lose everything, and there was nothing we could do about it.

No. I wasn't going to let this happen. If Brenda was released, she would be able to handle everything at home. I decided internally: I'm going to handle this differently. They need to get me and let the rest go. I'm going to tell the truth. Without a second thought, I stood up.

The judge frowned, and asked, "Was there something you wanted to say?"

Yes, I wanted to say something. My Portuguese was fairly good by then, so I stated loudly and clearly, "First of all. All these people who have been pulled into my case: I don't know them. The fact that these petty street dealers have been jammed into my case is a disgrace to who I am as a criminal. I'm a manufacturer, and they're just small-scale dealers. Again, I don't know these guys at all, and I would never sell them fifty or a hundred pills. I only sell pills in really big batches."

"And second. About my wife: if she doesn't do what I tell her to, I knock her across the room. She's forced to do what I order her to do. When I tell her: 'Go pick up the money!' she goes and picks up the money. If she doesn't, she has a serious problem! She only does what I tell her. Let her go!"

The judge glared at me angrily. "You've got some nerve!"

"No," I replied, "I'm not being rude, I'm just telling the truth. The only criminal in court here today is me. And if you want to punish someone, you should be punishing me! Don't let them be the victims of my crimes. You want me? Well, you got me. I'll tell you anything you want to know."

The message came across, loud and clear, and they seemed to accept it. Even so, they still questioned those other guys. The man who had given a statement that he had received pills from Brenda now stated – when I pushed him to tell the truth – that he had only given her money. Good. That new statement was a great help in Brenda's case.

After that they were done pretty quickly, and we were allowed to leave again, the same way we had arrived. What a circus.

Fourteen days, that's how long we had to wait before we could go back to court to hear the verdict. And it was exactly the outcome I had hoped for. The court nearly erupted! All the guys were let go, and Brenda was released immediately!

The only one who was convicted was me: sentenced to eleven years and nine months. We got everything back: our house, our cars, our jewelry, everything.

No, I wasn't going to file an appeal; I was happy, and relieved that I hadn't gotten twenty-five years! Plus, I was so happy that Brenda was free. She could be with the children. And the most important thing: we would be requesting a transfer to the Netherlands. The sentences there were much lower, and I would be out in a few years.

I thanked the judge and the lawyers thanked me, because their clients were free because of what I had done. Grinning widely, I walked out with the ninjas. They didn't understand it at all: that dude just got sentenced to almost twelve years in prison, so why is he smiling? Well, because it could have been a lot worse!

It was a huge hassle to get all our stuff back again. It turned out that our security camera system had been installed at the police station, and our furniture was no longer in secure storage, but in people's homes. They just stole it – 'borrowed', of course, but giving it back was apparently hard to arrange. Such a corrupt system. Bizarre to see how people profited from our misery when our lives were crumbling around us.

Brenda sold everything off as quickly as she could, including the house, and went back to the Netherlands. Finally she was with the children and the family again. That was a real load off my mind.

THIS POOR MAN
CRIED OUT, AND
THE LORD HEARD
HIM, AND SAVED
HIM OUT OF ALL
HIS TROUBLES.

PSALM 34:6

18

MADEIRA

Once I had been convicted, they no longer wanted to risk keeping me in a less than secure prison facility. They sent me to Madeira, a small island with the most heavily guarded prison in Portugal. No one had ever escaped from there.

On the way we made a stop in Lisbon, where I spent the night in solitary confinement. It was black as pitch in there; I had no sense of time and felt incredibly lost. I could hear rustling and squeaking all around me; vermin were not uncommon in those prisons. More than once, I stamped on the floor as hard as I could to shoo the pests away.

The next morning, the ninjas were ready and waiting for me, to fly me across to my new accommodations. It was a large prison, I could see that right away. There were four prison wards, with two small yards and two big yards in between where prisoners could go outside. That looked fine to me.

But a guard took me to a cell just for me, a bare cell with no extras at all. No radio or TV, and I wasn't allowed to make phone calls or receive visitors. I got a prison uniform to wear, and then I was number five. Not Johan anymore, just number five. They explained to me very clearly how things worked here and what the rules were. Then they left me there, alone in my cell.

What was this, some kind of quarantine? I thought I had seen it all, but this was new. The days passed slowly; the walls started closing in on me, and I gradually felt like I was going crazy. I would not make it like this, spending twelve years in solitary!

Luckily, that wasn't the case. Eight or nine days later, I was finally allowed to go out. The guard took me to a big cell with twelve men. That was a major change for me, but better than being so isolated.

There was a big yard outside, really gigantic, where we could play soccer. There were some small tables out there too; we could do fitness routines, and there were little mats to sit down and relax on, scattered all over the place. The mood was less intense than I was used to; the guys were more helpful. It was just fine!

But in the middle of the night they pulled me out of my bed again and transferred me to a different ward. What was this? I was back in a one-person cell, with no TV, no radio!

I didn't understand what was happening, so the next day I asked to talk to the warden. He explained it to me. "We made a mistake. See, that big yard, a helicopter could land there to pick you up. Since you're a flight risk, you can't be placed in that ward. The risk of escape is too high. This yard is smaller, so a helicopter wouldn't be able to land here."

Was he serious? "Well, I guess I'll just call the mission off then," I exclaimed sarcastically.

The advantage was that I had a cell to myself again. I decided to make the best of it, but I did miss having a radio and TV.

I heard some pretty heavy stories there. Literally intense, like when I walked past that one cell with the horrible stench. The guy in that cell was from a really tiny village on Madeira.

Madeira itself is a very small island; everybody knows everybody. Other inmates who knew what had happened told me that his mother had abused him, but she claimed that it was the other way around. And then he had been convicted and sent to prison for eight years. So heavy.

The guy had a mild mental disability and couldn't take care of himself. He never took a shower, he never cleaned his cell. He never even brushed his teeth – they looked all mossy and green, so disgusting! I could hardly talk to him without throwing up from the stench hanging around him and coming from his cell. This wasn't acceptable!

"No time for that, don't you know," the warden said when I asked him about it, "and he has to take care of himself. It's his own responsibility."

I gaped at him, astonished. "Are you serious? How inhumane are you people?!" But nothing happened. So I decided to do it myself.

I went to the kid and said, "Dude, I'm going to help you. I'll bring you a toothbrush, and shampoo and clean underwear. You're going to go take a nice shower and wash yourself!"

I sent other men to clean his cell. I really wasn't going to do that myself; it was too disgusting. Together, we dragged the filthy mattress out of the cell. It was too wet and disgusting to do anything with. I didn't want to know what was in there after all those years.

After that, the guards went ahead and found him a clean mattress. The walls were white again, instead of yellow, and we put in a TV. The whole cell got a makeover. The guy could barely understand what was happening to him, but I realized it made me really happy to do it.

I had never felt so satisfied in my life about giving anyone money or stuff. So I kept doing things like that, and it was fun for me.

If I'm honest, sometimes it was for my own benefit. There was this one guy who sat across from me at the table during meals, and he was driving me crazy. He only had one tooth left, so his eating habits were really disgusting, horrible to watch.

"Why don't you get false teeth?" I asked him, mainly so I wouldn't have to keep looking at that one lone tooth.

Grossly chewing his mouthful, he looked at me in surprise. "Do you have any idea how expensive that is? At least a couple hundred euros. Where would I get that kind of money?" he asked, spraying grains of rice from his mouth in my general direction.

Well, I definitely had that kind of money. "All right, I'll take care of it for you," I said.

And it wasn't just that one set of false teeth. A few months later, almost the whole ward had a gleaming white smile. Such a kick!

Of course there were also people who wanted to take advantage of me because they knew I gave stuff away easily. "Give me cigarettes now, or we'll stab you in the showers," they would say.

I don't think so. "I'll give whatever I want to whoever I want. I don't have to do anything, and you don't impress me, so if you want to stab me, you'd better do it now."

Luckily, other guys came to my defense, but it wasn't a pleasant situation. Those thugs kept coming by, and tensions stayed high.

It was completely normal to stab someone in there, so I stuck close to some other prisoners. By that point I had already gotten to know lots of inmates and guards. If I went to work out or if I had to go to the doctor, I would run into people from the other ward, and we'd often have a chat. I got along well with Pedro, a guy in my wing. It wasn't so bad, all things considered.

At Christmas we really threw a party. Everyone was allowed to arrange to have delicious foods brought in, which we were allowed to eat in a big room with our families. Any leftovers could be taken upstairs with us. Well, you didn't have to tell me twice!

IT IS MORE BLESSED TO GIVE THAN TO RECEIVE.

ACTS 20:35

My family brought along bags and bags of yummy stuff, like licorice, smoked fish, all sorts of things that we couldn't buy there. It was a wonderful Christmas dinner, and we had lots of delicious food to eat for a long time after that.

The guards could also see that I wasn't doing anything bad, that I wanted to help and was trying to be friendly. So after a while, I gave it a try and asked, "Couldn't I go back to that other ward, with Pedro? The guys in there are more laid-back, and there's not so much stress or drugs, the way there is here with these young, aggressive kids."

The warden thought it over for a couple days, and then let us transfer to the other wing. It was great.

That's not something that I would have been able to arrange in the Netherlands. Since the warden knew Pedro and his family and I was hanging out with the guy so much, we were able to make it happen. This place was much less strict; if you knew the right people, you could get a lot done. It was corrupt sometimes, but it could also be really nice when things worked out well.

After my transfer I kept on giving things away, and I discovered how happy I was just being myself: a fun, friendly guy not looking for trouble, a guy who doesn't want to profit from people, but who helps people and treats everyone with respect.

For the first time, it seemed like people were also being sincere with me in return. Not because of what I had, but because of who I was as a person and how I interacted with others. Not that I wanted that pat on the back to be good enough, although that was still in there somewhere too. This way of being, of doing right, just made me really happy. It gave me a lot more satisfaction than the way I had lived before.

And I also heard personal stories about the consequences of drug use, drug dealing and crime. More and more I started seeing the bigger picture, realizing how drug trafficking was an instrument of evil, and how the world ran on that fuel.

Above all, I realized that there was a whole different world out there, separate from this scene. Not everyone was in prison, and not everyone took drugs. What was that other world like, the world I didn't know? What would it be like to live in peace and quiet and have a normal life? That used to seem stupid and boring to me, but by that point I was curious about it, possibly even longing for it.

In the meantime, I still had to face hard reality: after this prison sentence, I still had to serve more than six years in the Netherlands. I wasn't going to be leading a normal life anytime soon. I was changing inside, but I didn't have a chance to go deeper because I was constantly surrounded by people. There was activity all day long; I was never alone. Those were long, lonely years surrounded by so many strangers.

Our two-person cell already gave me more peace and quiet. Watching TV together and talking a bit, very laid-back. Just looking away for a moment when the other needed to use the toilet, but other than that, it was fine the way it was.

I beautified the cell a bit by hanging a cheerful, colorful cloth on the wall and sourcing some Christmas lights. Considering the circumstances, I was doing pretty well.

Brenda regularly came down from the Netherlands to visit for a whole week, even without supervision, although we weren't married. The management knew how much we shared, and they allowed it.

By that time, I had been there for nearly four years. My request for transfer had been delayed because more charges were pending against me for giving a false name when I was arrested.

Such a disappointment when I discovered that! Otherwise I would have been back in the Netherlands two and a half years earlier. That made it even more nerve-wracking to keep waiting.

All the time I was walking on eggshells, because the slightest slip-up would get me even more hassle, and then I wouldn't be able to leave after all. If someone hated your guts and tossed a chunk of hash into your cell, you'd be back in court and not going anywhere.

No matter what it cost, I wanted to avoid being here for eternity, so I was on my very best behavior, trying hard not to stand out, and avoiding any additional charges. It was incredibly stressful.

Every day was a struggle to survive. Every day. Staying alert, never letting your guard down for a second, because evil lurked around every corner.

FOR WE DO NOT WRESTLE AGAINST FLESH AND BLOOD ... BUT AGAINST SPIRITUAL HOSTS OF WICKEDNESS IN THE HEAVENLY PLACES.

EPHESIANS 6:12

AND YOU WILL SEEK ME AND FIND ME, WHEN YOU SEARCH FOR ME WITH ALL YOUR HEART.

JEREMIAH 29:13

19

FINALLY ON MY OWN – BUT NOT ALONE

My cellmate was released. Great for him, good for me too, because now I was alone in my cell. Once again I had managed to get my hands on an unauthorized cellphone. Finally I could have an uninterrupted video call with Brenda. I would be able to see her eyes, her face. And the kids would be able to wave at their dad. Thousands of miles apart, but still close for just a few moments: gazing up at our North Star together and talking to each other.

I also had a lot more time to think about things. What kind of life was this anyway? And above all: what kind of life had I been living all these years? Why would I want to hurt someone, mess up their life, just for money? Wouldn't it be so much better to help other people instead of using them?

These thoughts were completely new to me, and just about short-circuited my brain. At the same time, I realized that I was thinking like a normal person for the first time ever. It felt like my heart had cracked open in the last little while. I kept searching for the cause; I was searching for more.

My gaze was frequently drawn to a picture of Jesus that was hanging on the wall. The TV was right next to it, so I looked at it really often, usually without being aware of it. It made me think of my own little statue of Jesus.

God still intrigued me, but I still didn't understand anything else about Him. Now it was like Jesus was looking at me from my wall while I sat there watching TV.

I had been watching a series on National Geographic about the discovery of the Dead Sea Scrolls. Someone wanted to sell them, but they were stored in a vault that wasn't airtight, so the paper was starting to crumble. There was no money to restore them or keep them safe.

As I watched the series with interest, I thought to myself: Why is this so incredibly important to them, to preserve these documents? Why is that text so fascinating? Someone came into the TV studio and gave an interview about the Bible, and for some reason I was powerfully drawn to it. All week long I watched the series every day, no idea why.

My head was filled with thoughts and questions. How did it all work: God, faith, life in general? I would often lie in my bed listening to music and thinking about my life. About what had happened, and more and more frequently about how I wanted to do things differently.

That evening was no exception. It was dark. The only light in my cell was the glow of my TV, and a little line of light from the hallway shining in under the door. To keep cockroaches and mosquitoes out of my cell, I always left the lights off so I could keep the little window open to let in some fresh air. The string of Christmas lights still added a festive note. I was lying there on my bed, lost in thought and listening to restful music on the radio. An ordinary, calm evening; it was nearly midnight.

Suddenly, I saw myself standing in the middle of the living room at Chantal's, my ex-girlfriend's place. It was so lifelike, so real; I wasn't in my cell anymore, I was *there*. We were fighting, Chantal and I, and our baby was crying in the background.

My mother was standing in front of me and she started talking to me. Our baby started crying even harder, and I heard myself say to my mother, "Now you shut up too, or feel free to let yourself out; there's the door!"

That was exactly the way it had happened, but now I could see much more. Now I could see the pain on her face. It was like watching her heart break right there and then. She started crying and ran out of the room. I stormed after her. I hated my girlfriend because the fight was making me talk to my mother that way. I grabbed my mother and kept saying over and over, "Sorry, sorry, I apologize, I didn't mean it, sorry, sorry, sorry!"

That evening in my cell, I lived through it again, and now I could only think: how could you hurt your mother so much by talking to her like that? I started crying, and called out loud: "Mom, never again, I'll never hurt you again, I'll never cause you sorrow again."

The words came from the deepest depths of my soul. The thought of her sadness was excruciating! I realized so clearly how much I had hurt her, not just in that moment, but all my life. She was always worried about me, always afraid for me. Now I felt her grief: so intense, so terrible!

That wasn't who I was at all! I had absolutely no intention of hurting my parents; I didn't want to disappoint anyone. I just wanted to be good enough, I wanted everyone to like me, that's all. There, at that moment in my cell, every bit of me crumbled into tiny pieces. Nothing was left.

And it didn't stop. One scene after another forced itself on me, nonstop. I clearly saw every moment when I had fallen short for Brenda and my children; how I had hurt someone's feelings by threatening them in a fit of rage; how I had manipulated someone to get my own way. I saw every single moment when I did people wrong for my own personal gain, how I had lied and cheated and betrayed people's trust. An endless flood of images flashed past, times when I scared people or hurt them.

Every scene was horrible! I felt their pain, fear, and sadness in my own body, like a punch in the stomach. What had I done?! Who had I become?! With every fiber of my being I felt ashamed, of everything: the reason I was in prison, everything I had ever done, truly everything. It was so much, such a heavy burden.

Gradually my sobs turned into screams. I beat myself on the chest and yanked my hair. I yelled: "Ahhhhhhhh, why, why, why?!"

As I sat there crying and calling out, I seemed to be grabbed by an invisible force. Before I knew it I was suddenly lying on the ground. What? How did I get here? What was going on?! I tried to get up so I could lie down on my bed again, but I couldn't! It felt like I had a ton of weight on top of me, like I was nailed to the ground. Whatever it was, I couldn't get up.

I lay there curled up in fetal position, my face turned toward the floor and buried in my hands. The only thing I could do was cry, cry, cry. The tears I wept came from deep inside me, from the bottom of my soul.

Suddenly, I felt something that hadn't been there a moment before. When I turned my head to look, I had to squint against the glare. It was like the sun was shining in my cell, such a fierce light, so bright. But it was the middle of the night! I thought I was going crazy. What was this?

As the tears kept pouring down my cheeks, I looked up again and felt the light completely surrounding me. My whole cell was filled with it! And I knew, I knew, I knew... God was in my cell! God was in my cell! It was simply incredible! He was in my cell! MY cell!

The realization overwhelmed me and made me feel terribly small. All I could think was: why? Why here with me?! Why would You come to ME? I've done all sorts of terrible things in my life. Unworthy, that's how I felt; truly a cockroach, a urine stain, a puddle of vomit. So awful, so worthless, so filthy.

And yet, You were there! Who was I that I would be allowed to see this, allowed to experience it, allowed to feel it?! It was a love so deep, so indescribable, so intense, washing over me like a flood, exploding around me: I simply couldn't comprehend it! And I didn't feel any condemnation at all. There was no anger, no rage, no finger-pointing, none of that at all. Just pure love.

And then it was like something said to me, "Ask Me." Not out loud; it was more a feeling of: say it out loud. It was like I had to give God permission to enter into my life. Don't ask me why, but I knew it. And I could only shout out: "Forgive me, Lord! Forgive me, forgive me!" That was all I could manage, and I must have said it a hundred times; I shouted it at the top of my lungs with everything in me.

As I shouted out, over and over: "Forgive me, Lord forgive me!" The love that filled my cell – God's presence, the Light – was inside me! All the way through me, like a sea of unconditional love washing me completely clean. And I heard a soft voice saying, "I forgave you a long time ago."

I wasn't in the cell or in prison anymore, but in a place I couldn't describe. It was like being in heaven. I was flooded with a sense of mercy and love I'd never known before in all my life. It was a supernatural, amazing experience, and at the same time I felt so unworthy. It was insane! It knocked me right off my feet. It broke me. This was so much more love than I deserved! And yet He was there.

Just a few moments ago I had felt a ton of weight pinning me to ground; now I was as light as a feather. It was like I was floating, so light, so free. Still, I stayed on the ground, weeping... but now they were tears of joy.

I kept calling out: "My God, my God, so beautiful, my God!" I hardly knew what I was doing or saying or feeling. And yet it was real: the Light, the Love. That sense of oneness with Him, the One I did not even know, the love I felt; it was so intense, so real, so deep! It felt like I had died and was being reborn; the sadness of death and the joy of new life; the depths and heights that hurt so much, and at the same time brought so incredibly much joy.

Delirious with delight, I lay there on the ground for hours, wiping the tears from my cheeks every now and then. Taking a while to recover, just for a bit... and BAM, there I went again, crying fresh tears

AND SUDDENLY A LIGHT SHONE AROUND HIM FROM HEAVEN. THEN HE FELL TO THE GROUND, AND HEARD A VOICE.

ACTS 9:3-4

because of the presence of God within me. Not in my cell anymore, but inside me.

I could only think happy thoughts, only see hope, love, a future, a way forward... light. The road ahead of me was completely clear; for the first time I felt true freedom. The darkness was totally gone. The sensation was so liberating, so light.

Tears poured down my cheeks, because I had such a clear realization: I am not the same anymore! The fact that I was in prison meant nothing to me anymore; I wasn't even thinking about it. I was free!

That night I didn't sleep at all. Only then did I realize that God had always been with me, in all my darkest moments. And yet there was no condemnation! He had always protected me. Those times I had talked to that little statue of Jesus, He had heard them all.

He loved me even when I was doing everything He said not to do. It was God who freed me from my coke addiction when I prayed to Him for help. He actually heard me! He knocked the glasses from my hands and kept the dealer away from me! He worked a miracle in my life in spite of it all.

No rejection, just the overwhelming emotion: you are good enough for Me! It was the best thing that had ever happened to me; I had to tell my family as soon as possible!

Before the door opened in the morning, I was already standing beside it, ready to go out. The guard stood in the doorway, looking sleepy. "Bom dia!" he yawned. I looked at him in amazement, because he looked so beautiful, like the face of an angel! And believe me, the people in that prison are really not all that pretty. But right now he looked gorgeous.

"Wow! Jesus lives, and He loves you, and He loves me!" I said with a big grin. Taken aback, the guard gave me a surprised look.

I quickly walked out and discovered that everyone looked different. The faces of all those men were beautiful! It was like I had ended up in a whole different world. All the colors were different; even the sky seemed to be more intensely blue. I could hear crickets and birds and smell flowers, even as I stood there in the concrete prison yard. It was so intense, just bizarre!

With a big smile on my face, I walked over to the telephone and called Brenda. "Guess what happened to me! I met God, honey, I met God!"

HE HAS DELIVERED US FROM THE POWER OF DARKNESS AND CONVEYED US INTO THE KINGDOM OF THE SON OF HIS LOVE.

COLOSSIANS 1:13

"Oh, really? Mmm, that's nice." Her voice was scratchy, distant, not all that enthusiastic. She had just woken up, of course. "Great for you, sure, I'm happy for you. All right, can I go back to sleep now?"

"Yes, sure, honey, but it's real!"

"Yeah, yeah, that's great," she said again, probably just to get me off the phone. A good night's sleep is important too.

So I headed out into the prison yard. One of the guys out there was someone I had talked to before about things like this, so I told him what I had experienced. He was really enthusiastic, thankfully. "That's unusual. I've been spending some time lately reading the Bible and so on, and I believe He's real too."

Almost shouting, I exclaimed: "He *IS* real, man, for sure!"

After talking to him, I called my parents. Because my father once had his own moment with God, in a sense, he knew what I was talking about. Both of them understood that something had happened to me. They didn't know much about Jesus, but it was clearly something positive, so it was good for me, and they were happy about that.

Then I told the guards and the prison warden about it; I just couldn't keep my mouth shut. I could see them thinking: this guy has totally flipped.

No, man; I'm finally normal!

THEREFORE, IF ANYONE
IS IN CHRIST, HE IS A NEW
CREATION; OLD THINGS
HAVE PASSED AWAY;
BEHOLD, ALL THINGS
HAVE BECOME NEW.

2 CORINTHIANS 5:17

LOST AND FOUND

Luke 15:11-24

A certain man had two sons. And the younger of them said to his father, 'Father, give me the portion of goods that falls to me.' So he divided to them his livelihood.

And not many days after, the younger son gathered all together, journeyed to a far country, and there wasted his possessions with prodigal living. But when he had spent all, there arose a severe famine in that land, and he began to be in want. Then he went and joined himself to a citizen of that country, and he sent him into his fields to feed swine. And he would gladly have filled his stomach with the pods that the swine ate, and no one gave him anything.

But when he came to himself, he said, 'How many of my father's hired servants have bread enough and to spare, and I perish with hunger! I will arise and go to my father, and will say to him, 'Father I have sinned against heaven and before you, and I am no longer worthy to be called your son. Make me like one of your hired servants.' And he arose and came to his father. But when he was still a great way off, his father saw him and had compassion, and ran and fell on his neck and kissed him.

And the son said to him, 'Father I have sinned against heaven and in your sight, and am no longer worthy to be called your son.' But the father said to his servants, 'Bring out the best robe and put it on him, and put a ring on his hand and sandals on his feet. And bring the fatted calf here and kill it, and let us eat and be merry; for this my son was dead and is alive again; he was lost and is found.'

And they began to be merry.

LET HIM WHO STOLE STEAL NO LONGER, BUT RATHER LET HIM LABOR, WORKING WITH HIS HANDS WHAT IS GOOD, THAT HE MAY HAVE SOMETHING TO GIVE HIM WHO HAS NEED.

EPHESIANS 4:28

20

STILL IN PRISON, BUT FREE AT LAST

My old life was over for good; I knew it, and I could feel it in everything. The money I had earned from selling drugs meant nothing to me now. I gave everything away: to prisoners who needed all sorts of things, like medicine, dentures, clothing, food, a television, a ticket to have their family come visit them, or money to send to their families on the other side of the world.

I gave money to a prison guard so he could pay off his debts, and I gave money to people outside the prison who were in urgent need. No matter who asked, for whatever reason, I gave everything I could give.

It made me feel incredibly joyous to see how happy people were about it. I finally felt like I was doing something useful with all the money I had piled up when I was in darkness. Before my conversion, I had already given lots away, but now it was truly selfless: no need for a thank you or a pat on the back. I didn't need anything from anyone; I simply had to do it, and it felt great. This was who I had become, thanks to Him.

Now that I had met God, I wanted to get to know Him better. So Brenda brought me a Bible, a thick book for me to read. But I didn't understand any of it.

I read: *"If your hand or foot causes you to sin, cut it off and cast it from you,"* Matthew 18:8. Cut off my hand? But I only had two hands...? The whole book was a complete mystery to me.

There was no one to explain it to me; I had to try to interpret it all myself, but I was completely unable to figure it out. I knew that the God of the Bible existed, and that Jesus was my Savior. But I didn't know exactly what 'Savior' meant. So I wanted to get to know Him better.

Even though I didn't understand much of it yet, I did know God's love for people, and I showed it. I talked freely to everyone, was open to everyone, and prayed with anyone who wanted to.

People started noticing that I was different from the rest. One kid came to me and said, "I don't get it. Weren't you sentenced to eighteen years in prison? But you're sitting out here in the yard every day with a smile on your face. You're really cheerful to everyone you meet. How is that possible? What do you know that I don't know?"

"God, man. That's what I know. Do you want to talk about it?"

As it turned out, his mother also went to church and often prayed for him. Jesus wasn't a strange idea to him. So I prayed with him too. "If you ask Jesus to forgive you, He does, and then He comes into your life."

Very simple, because that's all I knew at that point. I did know one thing: people were touched by it.

People kept coming to me: guys who were on the brink of committing suicide, guys who were seriously addicted to drugs, guys who were losing it at the thought of serving such a long prison sentence. I got to encourage them all. I told them about God, that He loved them and wanted to give them strength – that God could change their lives. Lots of them came to faith as a result!

Those beautiful experiences also encouraged me, even though I didn't have much knowledge of the Bible yet. I felt very free, because I had come to know the God of love, and was eager to pass that love on to others. "He's real, man, He really exists, and He is love!"

Once I got out of prison, I wanted to go to a church where everyone was happy; I knew that already. I really wanted to go to the church I had seen so often when I was a child. We used to play near there, and I could remember the text written so large that it covered the wall: "Jesus says, I am the Way, the Truth and the Life."

I had probably read those words a thousand times, but I didn't understand them at all, and I thought it was just some creepy building with a strange text on it. I had no idea what happened in there.

I didn't know anything about the different church denominations; I just wanted to go to a happy church where everyone was singing and dancing. The thought made me feel cheerful. Brenda went to that church a couple times and she told me it really was one of those 'happy churches'.

Brenda had always believed there was a God, but she had been baptized as a teenager mainly so she could get married in a church. She didn't have any particular attachment to church, but she thought those services were fine.

YOU ARE THE LIGHT
OF THE WORLD.

MATTHEW 5:14

DO YOU WANT TO BE UNAFRAID OF THE ONE IN AUTHORITY? DO WHAT IS GOOD AND YOU WILL HAVE PRAISE FROM THE SAME.

ROMANS 13:3

I wanted to go home so badly, especially now that I was both clean and free. But it would take a lot of time and patience before that happened.

I spent another year working on my WOTS[2], so I could be transferred to the Netherlands. The paperwork had to be translated, and everything had to be handed in to the Ministry of Foreign Affairs, Interpol, and everyone else involved. I wouldn't be able to return to the Netherlands until that all was arranged.

Finally the time came. I would be allowed to go to my wife and children and family! Not free yet, but much closer.

But they demanded even more patience from me. First, they had to arrange a flight from Madeira to Lisbon, since that was where I had to sign the paperwork in court. From there I would go to the airport and then back to the Netherlands. There was still a lot of hassle and bureaucracy, and I couldn't wait!

One morning someone came up to me and announced: "You'll be on the plane on Friday, flying back to Lisbon." It was really going to happen!

I gave all my things away and said goodbye to my friends there. No matter how eager I was to leave, it still affected me. They had been a part of my life. We had shared laughter and tears, and gone through stormy weather together. I had tears in my eyes as I said goodbye to some of the guys. It was painful, even though I was deeply relieved to be leaving that place behind me.

And then it was Friday. The day of days. D-Day. Or so I thought.

There was a delay that meant I wouldn't be able to leave until Monday. Those two extra days seemed to take forever.

On Monday I said goodbye to everyone all over again. The Special Unit was standing by, ready to escort me again: men wearing balaclavas, helmets and bulletproof vests, and carrying machine guns. They were my constant security escort when I had to be moved anywhere, even if only to the dentist.

Then they would first block off the whole street and clear out the building at the dentist's office. Next, three armed men would stand around the dentist while he drilled into my teeth, his hands shaking and beads of sweat on his forehead.

On that Monday they were leading me outside, out of the prison. I sat in the van wearing handcuffs, and the head of prison security said to me in English, "Johan, I've never met anyone like you in prison before. You're a good man, and I know that you've done many good things during your time in prison. I wanted to thank you for that. You made a difference. I'm sorry you have to be transported like this, because I'm sure if I had said to you: 'Walk to the airport', you would have done it." I had a lump in my throat.

In Lisbon I was placed in a high-security ward for long-stay prisoners, with cameras everywhere. There aren't cameras in every ward of every prison, so lots of things happen unseen in there. When cameras are installed it's because they want to keep an extra eye on you. That also applied to me.

After signing the paperwork in court, I waited there to continue my journey. "In six weeks you'll be going back to the Netherlands," the judge had said to me. I clung to his words, and the countdown started.

In the meantime, I couldn't keep my mouth shut about God there either. All sorts of beautiful things happened in that prison in Lisbon. A couple of guys came to Jesus as a result of my story, and I prayed for some of the people in there, who immediately saw an improvement in their situation.

Even the guards would send hopeless cases to me. So I was praying with people who were mentally ill, guys with suicidal tendencies and psychoses, but also major criminals who had committed serious crimes.

One of the guys, Pequeño, was in prison for murdering a drug ripper. Fearing for their lives, he and his buddies shot the guy who was trying to rip them off, and were planning to cut him into pieces. His buddies were acquitted, but he got 18 years. He was hardened by the life he had been living, and now he had to be strong in here in order to survive.

One day he was caught with a cell phone and had to go into solitary for thirty days. When he got out, scruffy beard and all, I walked over to him and went into his cell with him.
He burst into tears and asked if he could find the same strength and joy that he saw in me. He couldn't understand that someone like me, who looked like just any other guy from the criminal underworld, could be such a soft and gentle man who wanted to help everyone.

I told him that God had made me that way through His love, and that He wanted to do the same thing for him. Weeping, he poured his heart out, telling me how ashamed he was of what he had done, and we prayed together for peace and calm in his life. Pequeño would get there, I truly believed that.

But no matter how beautiful that time was, by that point I really wanted to leave. Six weeks had turned into eight, and nothing was happening. I couldn't understand it. When I called Brenda and complained, she told me I should call the WOTS office. That was a good idea; then at least I would know what to expect.

The person I ended up talking to on the phone was clear, but what they had to tell me was something I absolutely did not want to hear: "You aren't coming back to the Netherlands."

"What you mean, I'm not coming back to the Netherlands?"

"All the papers are in order, except for the case you were prosecuted and sentenced for in Portugal, for giving a false name. That's not a crime that would be prosecuted in the Netherlands. We can't transfer that sentence, so you'll have to stay there."

What? As a serious drug criminal, armed and dangerous, they were willing to take me, delighted even, but giving a false name meant they couldn't take me back? Man, that was a sentence of two months! I had been in prison for five and a half years; hadn't those two months been served by that point?

That decision meant that I would have to spend twelve years in prison here first, and then serve the other sentence in the Netherlands. It couldn't be true!

It was so intense after everything we had already been through. Brenda was completely shattered. There was no way we could make it that long, but it didn't seem like anyone could change anything about it. The decision had been made.

Deeply disappointed, I walked back to my cell, picked up that heavy Bible, and opened it. My gaze fell on John 15:7. It said: *"If you abide in Me, and My words abide in you, you will ask what you desire, and it shall be done for you."* I read it a second time. *"If you abide in Me, and My words abide in you, you will ask what you desire, and it shall be done for you."* And I read it again. And again.

BAM! It was like God had poured it into my heart like a revelation. I almost shouted it out: "Lord, I DO abide in You! And You abide in me. And what I want is a miracle. Aren't you a God of miracles?!" What I want to ask isn't a hamburger or anything. No! It says here: ask what you desire and I will give it to you. Like God Himself was saying: go ahead, ask.

So I asked, "I want a miracle, Lord. I want to go back to the Netherlands. I have given everything away, I've done what I could. I told people about Your love and I did good things. Now I don't want to be here anymore!"

Silence. I felt a sense of peace, but there was no answer. Now what? How long should I wait?

That evening I fell asleep around eight in the evening. I normally never managed to drift off that quickly. When I woke up the next morning, I could feel it immediately: something had changed. There was an enormous sense of calm within me.

I walked downstairs and, as always, called Brenda first thing. "Good morning! How are you doing?" she asked.

"I'm actually doing pretty well! I don't know why." Brenda was still really bummed out, and I could understand it. I tried to cheer her up: "I prayed last night, and..."

Just then, a guard tapped on my shoulder. "Johan, sorry to interrupt, but do you have any money left on your card?"

"No, I don't," I replied. "Why?"

"Oh, you're leaving on Monday."

"Brenda, hang on, I'll call you back in a minute." I hung up and asked the guard, "Where am I going?"

"I don't know," he replied, "but I'll find out for you."

I was nervous. What if I had to go back to Madeira to serve the rest of my sentence there? But he returned quickly and said, "You're going to Holanda."

"Holanda?"

"Si, Holanda, Monday."

Really! See, something had changed! I fell to my knees and said out loud, "Father, thank You for being such a good God. Yabadabadoo! Hallelujah!" The guard looked at me like I was crazy, but I didn't care. I was so happy, I called Brenda right back.

"You'll never guess! Monday I'm coming to the Netherlands!"

She screamed down the phone line, "Really, are you serious? Is it true? I'm going to call the WOTS!"

"No! Don't call! Please! This is a gift from God. Don't call!" What if they changed their minds!

The weekend seemed to last forever. So nerve-wracking! What if it wasn't true after all? The Ministry of Foreign Affairs had been very clear: "You aren't coming back to the Netherlands." Period! And now someone was saying, "You're going!" What had changed?

Finally it was Monday morning, and I packed my things as soon as I got up. Those guys with their helmets and balaclavas and bulletproof vests were back again. Well, I was definitely going outside, that was for sure, because they were there for a reason.

They searched me again. For the umpteenth time I stood there naked, but none of it mattered to me anymore. One day that humiliation would be over too.

It was sweltering hot, at least 95°F. When I got into the stuffy van, I saw another Dutchman sitting there. I looked at him, and he looked back at me. "Hey," I said.

"Hey," he said back.

"Are you going to the Netherlands?"

"Yes, how about you?"

"Yeah, me too, man."

"Cool! I got lucky," the man said. "I got someone else's spot. The other guy was supposed to go back, but he ended up not going. So now I get to go back in his place."

The man who wasn't going back, I realized, must be me! That was about me! But of course I didn't tell him that. That made the situation even more nerve-wracking for me, although I tried to hide it well. "Oh, that's too bad for the other guy," I said. "And really cool for you!"

The van left for the airport a bit later. I was drenched in sweat – from the intense heat, but also from the tension of waiting. Once we got to the airport, the van stood there unmoving for hours. The windows were blacked out; we could only see vague outlines through the narrow seams along the edge. It took so terribly long. I was terrified that something was wrong after all. The guy next to me kept saying, "I don't understand why it's taking so long. This is really weird." Oh man, don't do that. I couldn't handle him starting too.

I could see shadows of the men standing outside waiting, but nothing else was happening! Obviously they must have figured it out. I would almost certainly have to go back to the prison. "Please, God, please, don't let it go wrong."

Finally, finally, the door slid open to reveal a short man standing right in front of me. Blond hair, blue eyes. The man was definitely Dutch, and no mistake. He spoke to the other man first, and then to me: "Good afternoon. Mr. Toet?"

"Yes, that's me."

"How are you?"

"Well, a little warm."

"Sorry it took so long; we were sorting out your tickets. It didn't go quite the way we had planned, but we managed. We'll be heading to the airplane now, and these are your instructions."

BUT JESUS LOOKED AT THEM AND SAID, 'WITH MEN IT IS IMPOSSIBLE, BUT NOT WITH GOD; FOR WITH GOD ALL THINGS ARE POSSIBLE.'

MARK 10:27

First he explained the rules to the man beside me, and then moved on to me. "Two men from Europol will take you up to the cabin. One of them will sit by the window, then you will sit beside him, and then the other man will sit on your other side. Do not make contact with other people on the plane, and do not cause a scene. If you're behaving, your handcuffs can come off. As soon as you make any trouble, your handcuffs go back on again."

I was fine with anything. "Sure, I'll do it." Meanwhile, I was thinking: go on, go on!

The van drove forward a short distance and stopped in front of the plane. We were let out, and I walked up the boarding steps, looking around. All sorts of emotions were passing through me. Was this really goodbye?

I kept walking up the stairs, into the plane, and sat between those two men. Still on my guard, still not certain that this was actually going to happen.

The doors closed and the aircraft started moving. Yes, yes, yes! I couldn't imagine that they would stop the flight now. I felt happier and happier, and when the plane's tires lifted off the runway and we were in the air, a happy tear ran down my cheek. I was really heading back to the Netherlands. It was a miracle! Thank you, Jesus!

I struck up a conversation with one of the Europol men. He asked how long I had been in prison.

After a few sentences, I started talking about God. Enthusiastically, I told him about God's love for everyone. "He loves you too! He wants to help you too!"

To my surprise, the man became intensely emotional. The tough Europol agent broke down, because of God's love. Of course that wasn't permitted on the job, so one of his colleagues came over right away and switched seats with him.

"Don't say a word to me," the new guy snapped.

"Sure, fine. God loves you too." I didn't say anything else after that.

The flight went by quickly and I could hardly contain my joy. As we approached the Netherlands and headed down for the landing, I looked out the window and saw the sun breaking through the rain clouds. A double rainbow appeared over the airport, and it was like God was saying to me: "Welcome home."

No words can describe what I was feeling at that moment. So beautiful, so incredibly beautiful.

FOR WE CANNOT BUT SPEAK THE THINGS WHICH WE HAVE SEEN AND HEARD.

ACTS 4:20

They led us outside, and I was taken to a holding cell. There was nothing in the cell except for a thin plastic mattress. It was fine; anything was better than where I had come from.

It took some getting used to that no one woke me up every two hours all night, shining a flashlight through my cell window to check whether I was still alive. I had to switch gears any time anyone started talking, because I wasn't used to hearing Dutch anymore. When my cell door opened in the morning, I automatically greeted them with: *"Bon dia guarda"* and the guards looked at me like I was calling them names.

Slices of Dutch bread with real butter and cheese, refrigerated fresh milk instead of shelf-stable packaged milk: it seemed like a five-star breakfast after what I was used to. Even the better bread that I had bought myself in Portugal hadn't tasted anywhere near as good as the fresh-baked, sliced bread in the Netherlands. Over and over I thanked my Heavenly Father for bringing me back 'home' again, even if I wasn't home in my own house yet.

Two days later, I was brought before the public prosecutor. She had to officially take me into police custody in this case.

I knew the courtroom all too well. How often had I been brought here for extensions of my remand into custody, suspended sentences, and convictions. The hallway and cells smelled disgustingly familiar.

The guards' faces were still sluggish and tired; they had no passion for their work. They had to do exactly the same thing over and over, day after day. Open the door, close the door. "May I, do you have, do you know, when can I?" They heard those questions over and over from the people in the holding cells. And then a lot of cursing if the answer was "I don't know" or "no."

How often had I been held here, hoping silently to be allowed to go home? So many times the answer had been "no," and the only one to blame was me.

A completely different man was sitting in the cell that day. I knew that I was in the final stages of a price I had to pay. It was the consequence of my own actions. Then it would be over, and I wouldn't look back anymore, only forward. *"But one thing I do, forgetting those things which are behind and reaching forward to those things which are ahead,"* Philippians 3:13. So I stood in the small courtroom, my head held high.

The public prosecutor was sitting in a cubicle with only a table and a chair. She had a stern, icy look in her eyes. The first thing she asked, with a critical tone in her voice, was: "Mr. Toet, what are you doing here?!"

"What do you mean?" I asked innocently.

"Well, you weren't supposed to come back at all."

Ah, there it was. Stay calm, Johan. "Ah, but I'm here now anyway. What are you going to do, now that I'm here anyway?"

"We aren't going to send you back, but you should not have returned."

I grinned. "All glory to my God, because He has worked a miracle." She was clearly not as cheerful as I was – yet I was the one who still had to go to prison for several years, and had already spent several years inside. That made it even clearer to me that it wasn't circumstances that determined whether a person was happy; it was faith in God.

Shortly after, I was transferred to a House of Detention in the town of Zwaag. I was assigned a cell of my own and had a chance to recover from the stress of the past few days.

I had also been summoned to appear before the court in the matter of my previous prison sentences that had never been completed, and I received a court date for my Portuguese case.

On the day I went to court, I was excited, and felt strong and confident that the sentence would be lowered considerably. But whatever it ended up being, I had made my peace with it.

I was brought before the court. The prosecutor from the Ministry of Justice asked, "Do you regret what you did?"

Surprised, I said, "I got caught, I confessed, I was sentenced, and now I'm serving my time. What possible point would there be to say to you now, 'Yes, I regret my actions very much?' I regret many things in my life, but God has forgiven me, and that's what is most important to me."

"Well, don't think that you're going to get away with it that easily," she responded. "You have a history of serious crime, so you can be sure I'll be asking for the maximum sentence."

"If it makes you happy, you should go ahead and do that," I answered without hesitation. My trust was in God. He would take care of me and free me from any condemnation.

I wasn't worried about what would happen with my sentence. I was just happy to be back in the Netherlands. My family was close enough to hug again, I could see my children every week; that was all that mattered now.

I had the chance to say a few words to the court if I wanted, so I read out loud a letter I had written: "I understand that I need to be punished for my actions, and I agree with that. God has appointed you in this world to judge the crimes that I committed. I trust that you will be guided by right judgment and will hand down the appropriate sentence."

And I meant every word. I knew that God had forgiven me regardless; I was free of condemnation.

The court gave me the maximum sentence for the case in Portugal: eight years and six months. I still had another six years and six months to go on my sentence in the Netherlands, so once those were combined, the total was fifteen years. I would have to serve two-thirds of those in prison. I had already served five and a half years, so I still had four and a half years to go. I was still at peace with the decision, and continued to trust that my Heavenly Father would take care of me.

AND YOU, BEING DEAD
IN YOUR TRESPASSES...
HE HAS MADE ALIVE
TOGETHER WITH HIM,
HAVING FORGIVEN YOU
ALL TRESPASSES,
HAVING WIPED OUT
THE HANDWRITING OF
REQUIREMENTS THAT
WAS AGAINST US.

COLOSSIANS 2:13-14

21

NEW LIFE

I had to serve most of my sentence in Zoetermeer. I immediately started figuring out what I would do when I got out. I never wanted to go back to my old life.

For years, Brenda and I had been dreaming of getting married, but we had never managed to because I was a fugitive from the law. I wanted so badly for her to be able to take my name. Once I was back in the Netherlands, I knew I would be able to get married, in a ceremony in prison.

Through the social worker in the prison, I arranged to propose to Brenda officially in their office. When she was standing there before me, I was pretty nervous, even though we both knew what her answer would be.

In the end I went down on my knees. "Bren, we've waited a long time for this, and now the moment is here: will you marry me?"

"Yes, of course! I'd love to," she answered. Yes!

We were allowed to hold the wedding ceremony in the church sanctuary of the prison. Along with some of her family members and mine, it was a very beautiful afternoon. Brenda looked like a queen, and I felt like the happiest man in the world. We cut a cake, drank non-alcoholic champagne, danced, and prayed together, and for a brief moment everything felt fantastic.

When the afternoon drew to an end, we gave each other one long, final kiss, and then I had to go back to my cell all alone. It was the bitter pill after a sweet afternoon. But nothing could wipe that smile off my face. I knew this period would pass eventually.

While I was in prison, I attended the church services. They were organized by a traditional church. It didn't appeal to me much, the way they did things. It was about God and the Bible, that obviously did appeal to me. But I didn't really get clear answers to all my questions; I didn't hear anything about the Holy Spirit or miracles in that church.

I did have a special bond with one man who preached there. He tried to answer my questions to some extent, but the lack of guidance didn't really help me to make any progress in my faith.

I finally got a different translation of the Bible, but I still didn't understand much of it. Even so, I prayed every day, and I also started reading other books, like a book by David Wilkerson called *The Cross and the Switchblade*, about a gang leader named Nicky Cruz who came to Christ. I recognized myself in the radical conversions I read about, and felt encouraged.

Along with a couple of other guys who were believers, we started praying together in one of the rooms in the ward. But after a while we weren't allowed to meet like that anymore. But of course I kept talking to people about God, and told the other men about God's love for them. They couldn't stop me from doing that.

I didn't argue with anyone, I respected everyone, and I was ready and willing to help anyone. That way I was trying to serve the last part of my sentence as well as I could.

Time crawled past. By then it was 2010, and I only had a bit more than a year left to serve: the first six months in an open camp with home leave every weekend, and the rest on house arrest with an ankle monitor. After that I would be under light surveillance.

This approach would allow me to slowly reintegrate into society. Spending nine years imprisoned in a system that determined every aspect of my life had shaped and damaged me.

In Portugal everything had been horribly corrupt and chaotic, and you never knew what to expect. Guards were often drug addicts too; it had been very intense to live surrounded by people like that. I constantly had to be on my guard, so it was exhausting.

At the same time, the prisoners had a lot of leeway. When the weather was nice, we would all sit outside in the yard all day long, really chill. We shared in each other's misery; the inmates felt a strong sense of solidarity.

But prison in the Netherlands was highly structured. My door opened at eight in the morning and closed again at four in the afternoon. During that time there were activities, and if you weren't doing an activity you were locked back in your cell. You ate meals in your cell; no social interaction. Then you would go to work. Or the other way around: work in the morning and activities in the afternoon. That was it.

THEREFORE YOU ARE INEXCUSABLE, O MAN, WHOEVER YOU ARE WHO JUDGE, FOR IN WHATEVER YOU JUDGE ANOTHER YOU CONDEMN YOURSELF; FOR YOU WHO JUDGE PRACTICE THE SAME THINGS.

ROMANS 2:1

You were very isolated and dependent. If you ran out of toilet paper you had to press an intercom and ask, "May I have a roll of toilet paper?"

"Yes, when I have time."

"Could I possibly get an aspirin?"

"Yes, when I have time."

The guards often had a lot of problems at home because of their stress at work, and they took it out on the inmates. There was often a huge gap between the guards and the prisoners, and the whole situation was rigid and distant. Thankfully, I was able to communicate reasonably well with most of the guards.

When I ended up in prison, I had just been clean for a year. Before that I had spent fifteen years living in the bubble of drug addiction, far from reality, and surrounded by constant rejection.

Once I got clean, I tried to process things, but I couldn't because I was still recovering and lots of stuff was still happening. Then I was arrested, and my life and family were torn apart. That also caused a lot of damage. It had been my own fault, sure – but it was still traumatic.

I still had so much anger inside me. I couldn't express my frustrations about the system, because I'd immediately suffer the consequences. I also felt a lot of anger about all the times I had been betrayed. Since God had forgiven me, I also had to forgive all those people. I found that incredibly hard. Because of what some people had done, I had spent a really long time in prison, even though it was obviously also a consequence of my own actions.

And I hadn't been a good husband or father or son. I had to start working on all of that, and I couldn't do it on my own.

At the same time I was also experiencing a lot of anxiety. What should I do when I got out? I had never learned a trade, had no idea how I would earn money. I had no friends, no acquaintances, no one. Just my wife and my immediate family. There was no one I could really talk to about my pain and anger.

There isn't really anyone who does that in prison. They just ask, "Do you think you'll go back to your old way of life?" "Well, do you have a crystal ball? I don't."

As part of those final twelve months I requested sessions to process my traumas. I received talk therapy at De Waag, where they tried to help me deal with aggression. Sadly, the sessions didn't help.

Finally, I got to go on leave! Brenda picked me up on Saturday morning, and I was allowed to stay with her until Sunday evening. When I walked through the gate and could suddenly see for yards and yards, it was like stepping into a new world. For nine years I had been living between concrete walls, and now I was walking outside into a world that had changed completely. It was all so unreal. I was overwhelmed.

I could see Brenda standing by the car, as the prison receded into the distance behind me. One moment you're spending nine years in a high-security lockup like you're a danger to society, and the next they're opening the gate for you like it's completely normal. I got into her old car, so low, I wasn't used to that at all anymore. She had a telephone with internet access. Incredible! The last thing I'd known was slow dial-up internet on the computer...

Brenda took me with her to her rental house, a row house in a low-rent neighborhood, where she was living with our son – her house where I'd never been before, and was so curious about.

I wasn't overly impressed with what I saw. A big pile of dog droppings lay right beside her front door, and crude words echoed in the street. There were police cars driving around, and it was a really busy street with lots of traffic and noise. It was completely different from what I'd been used to. I had been living in a villa. With a swimming pool. And a big fence around it. What was this?!

It was a huge step for me, but of course it was also a big deal for my family, who had had to live without me all those years, and hadn't had an easy time of it. We tried to act like everything was normal, but I could feel the apprehension about what it would be like now I was home again.

Even before I stepped across the threshold, my son flew into my arms. "Daddy, do you want to see my room?" he exclaimed. He took my hand and pulled me with him. The interior was plain and minimalistic: small kitchen, narrow stairs going up.

We walked upstairs together. What a mess! But he was delighted. "Look, Dad, Star Wars and Pokémon, I got all these as presents!" Such a cheerful, enthusiastic child. We went back outside together and I spent some time playing with him. We went skateboarding and I intensely enjoyed being with him.

The small house gave me some idea of our financial situation, but I really had no idea yet. I had given everything away when I was in prison, but I had no idea how we stood now. Brenda worked hard, she had a fun job in healthcare, but she couldn't quite make ends meet financially. Because

MY PEOPLE ARE DESTROYED FOR LACK OF KNOWLEDGE.

HOSEA 4:6

she regularly came to visit me, I had thought everything was fine. She had never said anything about it, either.

Now I was discovering that it had taken her a lot of effort to keep her head above water, and that we were all out of money. In fact, we were several months behind on the rent, and the unpaid bills and other debts were piling up.

This was so different from where I had been before, when money wasn't an issue. We still had a long way to go. Our financial situation was a source of concern for me. Sometimes I worried that I would have to return to my old life to get things sorted out again. I didn't know enough yet about God's promises and what the Bible said to believe that everything would work out.

On Sunday morning I went to an actual church for the first time in my life: the church I knew from back when I was a child. I was excited and nervous, and I had no idea what to expect, but everything in that church was about God, so I was sure it would be completely amazing; I could hear myself thinking it.

As soon as we walked in, I felt God's presence. A warm glow washed over me. It gave me goosebumps. It was great! All those people worshiping God in that church, it felt so wonderful and so good! I had been longing for this.

All that time I had been alone. Of course I had talked to other people, but I had never been in a room with so many believers at once. Now I was immersed in God's love, surrounded by brothers and sisters. Such a warm welcome!

I introduced myself to the pastor and told him that I was in prison, but had come to faith. He thought it was great! "Super, I'm going to interview you! What a story!"

Brenda was also intensely affected by the service; I could see it in her face. When there was an alter call, I nudged her: "Isn't this for you?" She nodded, she could feel it too, and a moment later she stood up and went forward. They prayed with her, and in that moment she gave her heart to Jesus.

A few minutes later we were side by side again and I was completely happy. It felt like coming home. Now we belonged somewhere, even though I didn't know exactly what that meant. In any case, it was the family of God.

All these people were 100% honest, they all loved God, and they all shared His love. They were such sweet people; they looked so happy.

In prison I was just another criminal, and people usually treated me that way, too.

But these people couldn't see that I had been a crook and had just spent years in prison. They were simply friendly, even wanted to give me a hug. "Good to have you here!" They seemed sincerely interested in me.

I felt all warm inside because I was allowed to be part of the church. The preacher was super nice and charismatic. This was going to be our church; I didn't have to look any further.

I went to that church every time I was home on leave. During communion, they asked people to stand up if there was sin in their life. You had to confess your sin, and only then could you take communion. If you didn't confess first, then you would be eating and drinking your own judgment, they said – and that could make you sick or lead to an early death. So I stood up every time they had communion. I definitely still had some sins to confess.

They also said that if you wanted God to bless you, you had to give generously of your money and your time. If you wanted something big, you had to do something big for God first. You needed to serve. If you didn't, then you weren't a faithful servant and God wouldn't be able to use you.

You also had to be obedient to your pastor and to everyone he put in authority over you. You weren't allowed to disrespect the pastor's family. They were called by God, the men of God, and you had to come as you were told and obey them.

There was a prayer meeting every Wednesday, and you were supposed to be there, and go to the church service every Sunday. You were supposed to give ten percent of your income, and more. If you had nothing to do, you gave your time to the church.

Since I still knew almost nothing about the Bible, I placed myself under the authority of these leaders and their rules. Obediently, I went everywhere I was told to go. God expected it of me, so I did it. Of course I was still doing it to be good enough for God; that what I was best at.

Radical as I was, my actions were not always loving. If someone asked me, "If I don't believe in Jesus, does that mean that I'm not saved?", then I would say: "No, that means you're going straight to hell." That was my logic, my framework: "If you don't do this, then that will happen. If you do this, then something else will happen."

Very clear, very black-and-white. There was no middle ground for me; that wasn't how I worked. "That's what it says, so that's how it works!" I knew no mercy.

I talked to my family the same way, but they wouldn't put up with it. My brother and my father wouldn't even talk to me anymore. Our youngest daughter had lots of problems, but the way I talked to her about Jesus only drove her farther away from me. I didn't know how to convince her. Jesus was very clear, wasn't he, about right and wrong? Why didn't they understand that? Didn't they hear it in the church?

That's exactly what they heard, which was why they didn't want to go to church with me. I was inspired and enthusiastic about it. It was just extraordinary, the church from my old neighborhood; this was simply where I had to be. They heaped praise on me: "Ex-criminal who converted!" They said that frequently in the church services, too: "And we also have an ex-criminal here in our congregation. Right, Johan?"

I was almost their mascot, their property, or anyway that was how it felt. I wasn't very comfortable with it, but I was willing to put up with it. For God. I was willing to do anything for Him, and I was still happy with the church.

I was less pleased with our financial situation. We were deep in debt, and I had no idea how to make money. I didn't even know how I would find a job without any diplomas or work experience. Brenda didn't earn enough and didn't always get her salary on time. And when she did, it was gone right away because of the debts. But I still wanted to be able to take my family into town to shop for clothes, go out for dinner, or just go away for the weekend.

I really only knew my old way of making money. I was well out of the crime world, obviously, and I knew that I didn't want to step back into that life. But now I was on the outside and I was being tested.

Someone from my old life came to me with a great deal. He looked at me hopefully, trying to persuade me that he had an unheard-of opportunity to make a lot of fast money.

I recalled how much money I had helped this old friend rake in before, when he was working for me. He was the only one of all my former acquaintances who had brought money to my family every now and then when I was in prison, and now all the money was gone because I had given it away.

In his eyes I could see the hope that the Johan he knew before was still there, the Johan who could make money and knew a guy for anything you could imagine. I didn't have any money at all, and I had been out of the scene for years, but my reputation was apparently still solid when it came to doing serious business. His words were so familiar to me. "This is easy money, no risk, a golden opportunity. You'll get in without any trouble."

The words blurred together; they were so familiar, in a world that I knew like the back of my hand. It would just take a few steps, and then it would be cash or jail. The story never changed; the motivations never changed. I was so tired of that life.

But what else could I do? I didn't have any other skills, I had nothing left, and I was living in debt in a bad neighborhood. My status, my lifestyle, my identity: all of it had been erased. I wanted to give my family everything, but I had nothing to give. I couldn't see any solutions; I had no opportunities. No one told me: "This is what you should do." I only knew one way, and it was this way. "Do what you have to, because no one else is going to do it for you," was my motto.

"Johan?" I looked up, startled out of my train of thought. "Are you listening? My client wants to have four hundred kilos of cocaine every month. There's no risk in terms of money; you'll get a hundred thousand euros every week, that's a thousand euros per kilo. All you have to do is help them make contact. Your contact wants to supply it and my contact wants to buy. He's got plenty of money. It doesn't get better than this, right?"

It all sounded so nice and easy. I nodded and listened to his arguments in favor of doing evil. It could go fast and make a lot of money; all the pieces were in place. But I knew from experience that nothing ever works out the way you want it to in actual practice, and that you don't get anything for nothing. "Let me think it over."

On my way home, it just kept playing over and over in my mind. I could do this. Even if it just went well a couple of times, I would have more than enough to start over again. It could solve all my problems. Or make more trouble for me. Would things be different this time? I didn't have to be the biggest anymore; I just wanted to earn money to have a future with my family.

Then my thoughts suddenly spoke to me, loud and clear. Johan, seriously, are you really considering this? Have you forgotten where you just spent the last nine years? Have you forgotten that you gave everything away precisely because you didn't want to do this anymore? Have you forgotten what God has done for you?

I answered my own thoughts: "I don't want this anymore! It doesn't feel right at all, but I don't know what to do. How am I supposed to take care of my family and lead a normal life? I don't have anything and I can't do anything. I don't see any way out of this miserable situation without money!"

My head was spinning from the struggle. I knew I didn't want this. I also knew I didn't have any other way out right now. "God, help me! I don't want to go back to the way things were!"

And then I heard God's voice: "Open your Bible." It was clear, and I simply knew I had to obey. I wasn't reading the Bible every day; I still didn't really see the point of it. I knew about God and Jesus, but I still didn't really understand the Bible.

"Open your Bible."

"Yes, OK, I'll do it in a bit."

"Open your Bible."

"...OK, I'll do it now. Man oh man..." Once I got home, I opened my Bible and saw Matthew 6:33. *"But seek first the kingdom of God and His righteousness, and all these things shall be added to you."*

"What?!" I was on fire in an instant, just like I had been on the day that I read in John 15:7 that I could ask Him anything, and a few days later I was miraculously back in the Netherlands. I had another revelation. Boom! Straight to the heart, like I was exploding!

God said to me: "If you trust Me, if you seek My Kingdom and seek to know Me, then I will give you all those other things. I know what you need. Don't worry about that."

Wow! It was real; He was here! I danced in amazed delight because He was talking to me! Because I didn't know the Bible well yet, I wasn't able to easily tell the difference between lies and the truth. Unlike Jesus, I couldn't refute a lie with the words, "It is written...", like in Matthew 4:1-11. I had no idea what was written.

God was asking me to trust Him with something I couldn't touch, couldn't see. It was a frightening, unfamiliar world out there. Certainty I knew: family, need money, now!

But God was saying to me: "Don't go back to your old ways. I pulled you out of that; trust Me!" Wow! I still couldn't see Him, but I could hear Him loud and clear!

I broke down and gave in, saying, "Lord, this is really scary for me. But even if I end up sleeping under a bridge without so much as underwear to call my own, I will never go back to that path. I will take this unfamiliar road and trust You. Show me, Lord."

TRUST IN THE LORD WITH ALL YOUR HEART, AND LEAN NOT ON YOUR OWN UNDERSTANDING; IN ALL YOUR WAYS ACKNOWLEDGE HIM, AND HE SHALL DIRECT YOUR PATHS.

PROVERBS 3:5-6

It was truly another conversion moment. A clear choice to do things differently. No matter what: no going back! I knew it with complete certainty, just like I knew for sure that I wasn't going to smoke tobacco or coke again. Indescribable. It was a determined decision, from the deepest depths of my soul. I started crying, and a huge sense of peace fell over me.

The next day, I went to the guy who had offered me the deal. I said, "Look, I gave my life to Jesus. God spoke to me and told me that I have to trust Him, so I'm not going to go along with your proposal. If you bump into me in the street after this, you don't know me. We're going to say goodbye now; that's it. You never have to contact me again, and I'll delete you from my contacts. This is where we go our own separate ways. That's the end of it."

He was completely taken aback. "Yes, but we could earn so much money! And then you bring Jesus into it? Come on, man, we all need this?" he tried one last time.

It was clear that he didn't understand what it meant for me to believe in Jesus, so I calmly explained what had happened to me. He was happy for me that I had found something that gave me peace, and he could see that I meant it. But he still thought it was a shame that I wasn't willing to join in anything anymore.

We shook hands and said goodbye. "All the best," he called out to me as I walked out the door, never looking back.

It didn't matter to me anymore what anyone else said; what God said was much more important. Time for a new season.

Within a month our situation had changed radically. Someone offered to let us rent his spacious home in a quiet area, and for the same price as our row house. Fantastic!

I wanted to get out of that neighborhood, away from the crime and aggression, the drug abuse and the behavior that went with it. It reminded me too much of my own past. Curses flew back and forth from one house to the next. I didn't want to be stuck in the middle of that with my family, and now I had a chance to leave.

Brenda's work was also going a lot better. Everything was headed in a new direction. God told me to trust Him, and I did. That decision was apparently enough; He knew I trusted Him. He clearly showed me that He was a God of His word.

We were earning a reasonable income by then, and trying to pay off the debts. But it was so much. I had my ankle monitor on and was allowed to work certain hours. I did maintenance work at a trailer park. I was off on weekends, but I still had my ankle monitor on then too.

It took me longer than expected to get used to living free again. Every moment outside was so intense for me, the impressions had such a strong impact that my senses constantly went haywire. When we drove somewhere in the evening, I'd only see the headlights, not the road. I couldn't understand how people could drive like that without getting into accidents! I hadn't been outside after dark in nine years.

Every weekend I was allowed outside, I was buzzing with adrenaline the whole time, and off-kilter for the rest of the week from processing the impressions of the fast-paced world and all the noise around us.

Every week I checked in with my probation officer. I was still struggling with fits of anger and panic attacks. I would think to myself: see, I'm never going to be okay again. I felt very strongly that God hadn't forgiven me for everything. He had allowed me to experience His freedom, but since I had started going to that church and was expected to confess my sins before communion, I kept thinking: surely He couldn't have forgiven me for *that*.

As a result, my past kept gnawing away at me. Once a sinner, always a sinner. So I would stand up at every communion service to confess my sins. I would often stand there all alone, surrounded by four hundred people who stayed in their seats. Wow, so all those people were pretty holy!

Again I felt that sense of rejection. Rejected by God, by the preacher, and by everyone. It was the same story all over again. Yes, I had watched a porn video, gotten angry, used swear words... so I had to stand up again. And the rest stayed in their seats.

Would I ever get there, I asked myself in desperation? I insisted that my family did the same. We all had to go to the church, or we were backsliders. We had to go to the prayer meeting. God required it of us. At least I thought He did.

AS FAR AS THE EAST IS FROM THE WEST, SO FAR HAS HE REMOVED OUR TRANSGRESSIONS FROM US.

PSALM 103:12

22

FREE AND YET NOT

It was the end of 2011 and I had finally served the last of my sentence. The ankle monitor came off, and the probation officers stopped tracking me. I also said goodbye to the Waag, where I had been going for my sessions. I didn't have to answer to anyone anymore; I was a free man.

Ten years of my life: that's what I paid for the crimes I had committed. Finally I could really try to make a fresh start, and I was completely ready.

Brenda had a job and we lived off her salary. When the church asked me if I would be willing to work as a volunteer in their kitchen, I said yes. "How often can you come work here?"

"Well, I'm available five days a week."

So I started working five days a week in the kitchen. I was a pretty good cook, and they eagerly made use of my skills. I cooked for about thirty people every day, and I sometimes cooked for as many as a hundred and thirty people when there were events, working all on my own.

I loved it, working independently, and I felt like I was doing something important for God: serving His people a delicious meal each and every day, made with love.

I worked hard. We gave generously to the church, more money than we could really afford to give since we still had so many debts.

I did everything for the church because I was doing it for God. I followed all their rules. I did it, but it was also incredibly exhausting. In prison I had been completely free and at ease with God, and He was at peace with me. Now that I was free, it seemed like faith was trapping me.

More than anything, I wanted to serve God and know Him better. So I also started listening to sermons by other people, outside the church. Every day I listened to talks and read books that could help me. I told the preacher I was doing that, but to my surprise he said it would be better for me to limit myself to the sermons preached in this congregation.

BUT YOU SHALL RECEIVE POWER WHEN THE HOLY SPIRIT HAS COME UPON YOU.

ACTS 1:8

What? Wasn't I supposed to listen to God? It couldn't be correct that I would never be allowed to listen to anyone else, never hear another beautiful message about God, right? I didn't think that was what the Bible said, either, or at least I hadn't found verses that said anything like that.

My freedom was increasingly being replaced by obligation, and I wasn't sure that was what I wanted. I kept experiencing such rejection in the church, such a sense of condemnation if I didn't do what they told me to do.

God Himself gradually opened my eyes. During one of the church services, which still continued to affect me deeply, I said to God, "I want to know You."

As soon as I said that, I was in a different place. There was nothing but love there. It lasted two hours, nothing but love, and I wanted to stay there forever, in His loving, merciful arms. I sobbed constantly the whole time. It was like having another conversion; I felt a very powerful sense of God's Spirit.

From the moment I said, "I want to know You," God seemed to reveal himself to me more and more clearly. Through the Bible, and through other people. Among others, He led me to the teachings of Andrew Wommack, a Bible scholar from the USA who gives Bible-based instruction about God's great mercy and unconditional love.

Those teachings gave me so many insights and helped me immensely to understand things better. Some of the things I learned, I had already known deep down, but I couldn't express them yet because I didn't know enough about the Bible.

I started devoting myself to reading the Bible. I would read, read, read every single day, as much as I could. I wanted to understand! From nine in the morning until one in the afternoon, I would sit and do nothing but listen to teaching. I absorbed it like a sponge, and so much happened to me as a result.

I discovered that I had been justified by His grace, through faith. Grace wasn't something that could be earned, but was freely given. I learned that I had already been forgiven. Not just a little bit, but a hundred percent. The Bible says, *"Though your sins are like scarlet, they shall be as white as snow,"* Isaiah 1:18. And: *"I will forgive their iniquity, and their sin I will remember no more,"* Jeremiah 31:34. I was sanctified and justified, good enough, without anything I had done myself. That was true freedom.

All those questions I had been asking were now answered, all at once! It felt like God was pouring all that knowledge into me, along with His love. I was overflowing! I kept reading the Bible, and I couldn't get enough of it. It was as sweet as honey.

BEARING WITH ONE ANOTHER, AND FORGIVING ONE ANOTHER, IF ANYONE HAS A COMPLAINT AGAINST ANOTHER; EVEN AS CHRIST FORGAVE YOU, SO YOU ALSO MUST DO.

COLOSSIANS 3:13

We decided not to go to that church anymore because we didn't experience that sense of freedom there. It wasn't all that easy to find a different church, so we were on our own for a while. Leaving the church also meant the end of my work in the church kitchen, so I had a lot of free time on my hands. I was happy to spend that time listening to teachings and reading the Bible, learning more and more.

But God apparently still had more for me to learn in that church. He said to me, "You need to forgive those leaders; they don't know what they're doing." At first I was surprised by the task set before me. Then I realized that I was judging them just as harshly as they had judged me. I wasn't any better than they were. It was a painful realization.

I decided to forgive them. Not just them, either, but all the people who had ever wronged me in any way. With a sincere heart, I forgave everyone and was able to let it go and give it to God. I no longer felt any resentment, and that gave me a wonderful feeling of freedom.

Contrary to everyone's expectations, I went back to that church. I wanted to show them that God really is love, that there is another way. Bringing along a large bouquet of flowers, I went back to the church with Brenda and asked if we could come back. We showed deep humility. Simply because I wanted to obey God.

They were surprised. They forgave me for leaving, thanked me for the beautiful flowers, and allowed us to come back. Right away they also allowed me to go back to work in the kitchen. We were back. Not entirely satisfied with how things were going, but we were willing to accept it.

In the meantime, I kept changing because of everything I was reading and learning about God, and I was more and more able to explain what faith was, even to my children and family.

Our youngest daughter still wasn't doing all that well after everything she had been through in her life. She was depressed and cutting herself. In the past she hadn't been open to the way I had spoken to her about God. Now that I had changed, my words landed better.

I also struggled much less with fits of anger. Talk therapy hadn't helped me, but God's love brought healing. I became softer, more loving, and more able to accept people. And I was able to find more enjoyment in being free. My life settled into a regular routine. I was able to let go of the prison mindset and start to live freely.

Once when I was talking to our daughter about her problems, I said, "If you could take just one pill and be completely cured, would you take it?"

"Yes, of course," she said.

"Jesus is that pill," I said to her. "If you let Him in, your life will never be the same again. You'll be free."

This time around she was open to it. "Do you really think that's true?" "I know it is. Do you hope that it's true?"

"Yes, I hope it is."

"That's enough for Jesus. Hope springs eternal. Shall we pray together?"

"What should I do exactly?"

I called Brenda into the room and we sat down on the couch, the three of us. Folding our hands together, I prayed, "Father, thank You for sending Jesus to die for our sins."

Giggling, our daughter repeated the words. It was still so strange to her. Together we asked God to come into her life. Nothing happened, she told me, but I was so glad we had had the chance to do this together.

When she went to bed later that evening, she talked to God again, asking, "God, if this is real, what Johan is saying, then I want that. Let my life never be the same again." She started crying hard and in that moment, alone with God, her life changed; it became new again.

The next day I asked her how she was doing, and she replied, "I'm doing fine, thanks." We repeated that a few days in a row, and then she said, "Do you know that I haven't thought about suicide even once since we prayed together?" Normally it would have been on her mind every day. "I haven't taken any more pills, and I'm having happy thoughts!"

"Wow! God has set you free!"

With tears in her eyes, she said, "It's really true, isn't it?"

"Yes, it's really true."

But she was still sleeping poorly. Now that she had encountered God, I told her, "Go lie in your bed and thank God for a wonderful night's rest. Even if you don't sleep a wink all night, do exactly the same thing tomorrow. Speak His truth out loud, and He will give you a good night's rest."

She did, and from that moment on she started sleeping well! As soon as her head hit the pillow, she simply fell asleep. Amazing!

She stopped seeing the psychiatrist and quit taking the medication. She was completely free.

Not long after, my youngest son was arrested for stealing a game for his PlayStation. I was the one to go pick him up from the station, and I could see his downcast expression.

BEHOLD,
I MAKE ALL
THINGS NEW.

REVELATION 21:5

I immediately thought about how my parents must have felt every time I got caught – and how my mother had said to me, "Just you wait until you have children of your own."

I didn't want this for my boy; he should have known better. I was angry, mainly because I couldn't understand it. How could he do this after I had warned him? He knew how things had ended up for me, the best example he could have of what not to do. So why had he done it anyway?

I asked him if this was the life he wanted to live, and he shook his head no, looking pathetic. I asked him, "Would you like to pray together and ask for forgiveness?" He was willing to do that, so we prayed together in the car. We asked if Jesus would come into his life. Such a special moment!

Filled with joy, I shared the news back home, thanking God that two of our children had already 'accepted Jesus', as it's often called. We asked our son and daughter if they wanted to be baptized, and they did.

The very next baptism service, there they both stood on the stage, wearing white robes and looking nervous, about to enter the water and start a new life. I was as proud as a peacock.

My mother also came to the baptism service. She would come to church with us occasionally. She could see major changes happening in our lives, and she was very happy that we had chosen such a different road. I never felt she thought it was weird, or that it bothered her that we talked about Jesus all day long now.

My mother had been raised by nuns in a convent orphanage, and had some pretty traumatic memories from that period in her life. There was no love there, so when we used to joke about saying a blessing before dinner, she had always said: "I cook it into the food along with the potatoes."

But this approach to faith did appeal to her, which was why she came along every now and then. Of course she didn't want to miss her grandchildren's baptism service. I talked to her, telling her: "Mom, if you choose to follow Jesus, your life will also be so much better. He's truly waiting for you." She understood it, and decided to accept Jesus too!

Right after the service, when we went upstairs for coffee, I sat down with her in a quiet corner. We prayed together. I really couldn't believe it; my joy was complete! I announced it to everyone who was willing to listen. And I became hugely hopeful that the rest of the family would also come to faith.

After that I was so on fire that I walked around all day long with a big grin on my face. God was so, so good!

23

AN UNFAMILIAR ROAD

One beautiful day, I got up early to go for a walk in the woods. I saw the rays of sunlight through the trees and marveled at how God manifested Himself through His creation, time and again.

Halfway through my walk I sat down on a tree trunk to rest for a moment. As I kept my eyes focused on my Heavenly Father, my whole heart and body were filled with an enormous sense of gratitude and I could no longer hold back my tears. So much had happened in such a short time.

"Lord, You are restoring all things in my life. You are showing me now that I really don't have to worry, because You are always with me. I am learning to know You and trust You more and more."

I thanked Him for every miracle and blessing I had been privileged to receive so far, and it was a long list. In my mind's eye, I could clearly see the day He had come into my life, how He had been with me every step of the way, in fear, in conflict, in uncertainty. He restored my relationship with my wife, with my children and with my family, and He ensured that they were also touched by His love. He gave me a house, work and food, and He let me know His unparalleled goodness and mercy. He brought me good things in every aspect of my life.

In deep delight at all His blessings, I stood up again and began praising Him for His goodness. "Oh, great King, I will never be the same again, for You came and conquered me, You took my heart and my soul and made me new again. I have received forgiveness thanks to Jesus, and You have given me Your Holy Spirit. Who am I that You who are so great and powerful, You who are so holy and pure, should reveal Yourself to me, know me and want to walk with me? Father, I will never forget all that You have done for me, and I will praise You in all that I do, think or say. You have saved me, and You love me as Your son. Thank You, Father, in Jesus' Name!"

The joy and incredible gratitude I felt toward God nearly made my heart explode. I had never been so happy.

ASK, AND IT WILL BE GIVEN TO YOU; SEEK, AND YOU WILL FIND; KNOCK, AND IT WILL BE OPENED TO YOU.

MATTHEW 7:7

Then I felt that God started speaking to me. He showed me a number of things from my life. He had sent me back to forgive the leaders of that church, but I realized then that He hadn't intended me to rejoin that community. I should have waited for Him.

He wanted to travel a different road with me: I was to be an evangelist and travel all over the world preaching His gospel. I would visit many churches to preach there, and many people would be reached.

He also showed me an image He had already shown me before: I saw a crowd of people, vast as the sea, all with their hands raised in surrender to the living God. I was on a stage there, helping them to enter the Kingdom of God.

Wow. I felt almost embarrassed to be seeing these things, because they were so grand they seemed exaggerated, but God spoke to me clearly: *"Not by might nor by power, but by My Spirit, says the Lord of hosts,"* Zechariah 4:6. *"Not your work, but My work. Not your capabilities, but My grace and mercy. There are no limits to what I can do in your life if you will only trust Me and serve Me."*

I believed Him and gave myself completely to His words and the images He showed me. God said that it was time to leave that church for good.

I had given it all, visited every church service, celebrated every holiday, and obeyed in all things. God showed me that I had been trying to be good enough for the leader of that church, but I only had to be good enough for God – and I already was.

So we left that church again, for the last time. But what was I supposed to do next?

For some time I had been reading the Bible study books by Andrew Wommack. One of the books included a card showing the Bible schools he ran all over the world, known as the Charis Bible College. There was one in the Netherlands too. That sounded great!

I decided to go to the open day at the school. How exciting! At the open day I heard that the school offered a study program for five days a week. That was a lot.

After lots of thought and consultation, and encouraged by Brenda, I decided to go for it. "OK, Lord, here I am. I give myself to You. I will devote myself to going to Bible school five days a week for two whole years."

I started attending, and it was fantastic! During that first year,

I learned so much about God and His love. Everything started to make sense.

In addition to studying, I also visited prisons to speak there, and went out into the streets to talk with homeless people. Not as part of a school assignment, but just because I wanted to.

I truly had a heart for people no one else would reach out to; people who were misunderstood, broken and damaged. To those people above all, I wanted to show that they had a place and that God thought they were wonderful. I felt very strongly that I might be able to reach these people with my story better than someone who hadn't lived that kind of life.

Brenda had also been through so much, and she had a great heart for the women we came across. We would hand out little bags of toiletries with a card tucked inside saying "God loves you." That little card might very well be able to change their whole life.

I also handed out clothing, my own clothes sometimes, or I'd buy gloves, hats, scarves, and sometimes coats.

One day I spotted a kid who looked really nervous and jittery. He was wearing a T-shirt, nothing warmer, and by then it was really pretty cold outside. I waved him over to me, but I could see that he felt uncomfortable.

So I dropped everything I was doing and said to my son, who was with me that time, "Watch the stuff." I walked over to the boy and spoke to him. "Hey there, buddy, how's it going?"

"Not that great, but I'm thankful to be alive," he replied.

"What a great attitude, big guy, a lot of people could learn from that!" I said to him. He gave me an awkward smile. I told him why we were there, and said that we wanted to give him something too. "Yes, all right," he said. I quickly called to my son to bring over a bag of supplies. I handed it to the boy, and he looked at the contents in amazement.

"Is all this for me?" he asked.

"All of it. And aren't you cold without a coat?" I asked him. "Pretty chilly, yeah," he answered.

Without a second thought, I took off my own coat and gave it to him. He was completely taken aback by that. "No, man, you aren't going to give away your own coat, are you?" he stammered.

"Not just my coat. You can have my shoes too, and here's a couple tenners to go get something nice to eat. God thinks you're just wonderful!" He was deeply moved and didn't know what to say. "You don't have to say anything. Jesus just wants you to know Him as He really is: a very good God."

"How can I learn to know Him?" he asked me sincerely. I explained the gospel to him and asked him if he wanted to convert and accept Jesus into his life. And he did. We prayed together, and then I gave him a really big hug. He could hardly hold back his tears... And neither could I.

"I'm going to be off now, because my toes are freezing," I said to him, laughing. And we said goodbye and went our separate ways. Lots of beautiful things were happening, and I realized how happy it made me to be able to help people.

My youngest son often went along with me, and was very sweet to the people we met. I was super proud of him.

Brenda sometimes went along with me too, although she still found it a bit uncomfortable to talk about Jesus, just like that, to people she didn't know.

My mother supported everything I was doing. Every now and then she'd even contribute a bit of cash so I could buy more things to give away.

My dad thought it was all fine, but from a distance. He didn't mind that we were helping other people, but as soon as I started talking about the church, he'd say, "I don't like that stuff. You'll never get me into a church, all that funny business!" He had never been one to hide his opinions.

In the meantime Brenda and I had found a different church. This place was laid-back, and I didn't have to do anything at all right away. That was a good thing, for now.

Every week I would bring new people along to the service with me; I'd invite everyone I met to come along. Brenda would shake her head every now and then when we needed an extra car to fit everyone in, but we always had tons of fun.

My oldest son and his girlfriend joined us more and more often. Since I had been released from prison, I had better contact with him, and he would sometimes spend a weekend at our house. We were gradually getting to know each other better. He was a great guy.

One day, he and his girl were at our house and we were talking about faith again. The discussion went deeper and deeper, and eventually I asked them, "Do you want Jesus in your lives? Wouldn't that be great?" That was apparently the right question to ask just then, because they both nodded yes!

Not long after their conversion, my oldest son and his girlfriend decided to be baptized, and so did my mother. Together with a number of other people who had come to faith, we went to the church to have everyone baptized.

It was so beautiful to see my mother standing up there on the stage, dressed in white. In front of fifteen hundred people, she gave her testimony that Jesus was her Lord. She also told them how proud she was of her son, because she had come to know Jesus in a different way because of me. I had a lump in my throat and was so happy I could burst.

Then my oldest son walked onto the stage, gave his testimony like it was the most natural thing, and got a big round of applause. Man, wouldn't he be a great speaker! I could hardly hold back my tears. Just look at that: all those people who chose to follow Jesus and have now been baptized, even my own mother and my oldest son!

I wanted to experience that every day, to do it every day: bring people to Jesus. And of course preferably also my own father.

One evening my father and I were sitting on the couch together watching a nature show on TV, which he loved. He didn't notice, but I was taking a close look at the deep grooves lining his face, and at his wrinkled hands. His tattoos were so familiar to me. An anchor, a ship's wheel, a boat on the waves, and the name of his sweetheart on his knuckles. They told a tale of a hard-bitten sailor.

Here was the man I had had so much conflict with, but who I had grown to love so much that it hurt. The man I had seen as my enemy when I was a small boy had become my very best friend.

The man he had been no longer existed, and hadn't for a while. Where he had once fought his way through whole cafés on his own, he was now struck down so badly by emphysema, a lung condition that he had been struggling with for years, that he could hardly even walk to the toilet. I could see the hopelessness in his eyes when he suddenly glanced over and caught my gaze. As he struggled to take a breath through the oxygen tube by his nose, he said to me, "Johan, I can't do this anymore. I thought that was it for me. It was terrible!"

I rested my hand on his shoulder. His health had been growing worse for several weeks. He had even fallen to his knees once because he couldn't get any air into his lungs. The emphysema was starting to take a toll; any minor viral infection could be fatal. He didn't dare to visit hospitals, fearing infection. He'd been taking precautionary antibiotics for weeks.

In the past few months we had been talking a lot about life, about our ideas and about faith. Sometimes we'd play guitar together all evening. Sometimes we'd share stories with each other, from the distant past and more recently. Since I had decided to stop trying to convince people I was right about faith, we had grown incredibly close.

By that time he had often told me how proud he was of me, and that he loved me. Even if it had only been a couple of times, it was enough to erase all the pain of the past. I hadn't blamed him for anything in years. He was who he was, and he was also good enough. These days, I enjoyed being with him and we respected each other.

My mother was off to her bingo night. Rubbing my hand over his shoulder, I wanted only one thing, and that was to hold him. He kept repeating over and over how horrible it was that he would have to leave my mother behind. I promised him that my brother and I would really take care of her.

"But Dad, we're not planning to say goodbye to you yet, anyway; you're a tough old man," I said, squeezing his shoulder gently. I wanted so much to pray for him, but I was afraid he wouldn't want me to. I had learned at the Bible school that we could pray for the sick. And here my dad was, sick. He was seriously ill. I wanted to pray.

But my fear of failure and rejection apparently still played a major role where my father was concerned. So I just said goodbye to him and walked out the door.

But on my way out, I felt moved to go back to him. So I mustered my courage, walked back and rang the doorbell again. He opened the door and said, panting, "Did you forget something?"

I replied, "Yes, I did. If you'll let me, I would very much like to pray for you, Dad." I was so nervous!

He was quiet for a moment, and then he said, "Fine, but I'm not going to kneel or anything." I laughed a bit, because that was what he thought faith looked like.

"Dad, you don't have to do anything. You can just stay sitting, and I'll pray for you." He was fine with that.

A bit nervously, I laid my hand on his back. With tears in my eyes, I prayed with all of my heart: "Dear God, thank You for my wonderful dad. I know that You love him even more than I do, and that You don't want him to be sick. You say that as Your child I'm allowed to pray for the sick in Jesus' Name. My dad is sick. So every virus and every bacteria that's attacking my dad: I order you to vanish in Jesus' Name!"

The tears were rolling down my cheeks, and my dad was also very moved by the prayer. He thanked me, and we hugged each other tight. I was so happy that I had prayed for him; it felt great.

Only a day later, my father started recovering, and he felt much better in no time! In the year that followed, he was doing very well. He was a lot more cheerful and did things with us that he had never done before.

"Dad, we'd like to come to your house for Christmas."

"Sure, sounds great!"

"Oh really? I thought you didn't usually like all that?"

Now he thought everything was fantastic. I wondered if he knew something that we didn't know.

A while later, I was sitting beside him on the couch again. I had sent him some Christian songs, which he had listened to, and we were talking about them. He told me he had been so touched by the lyrics of a song that said that God knew him, his sitting down and his rising up. He meant Psalm 139.

I read the psalm out loud to him, and he was immediately enthusiastic: "Yeah, that one! Isn't it beautiful? God knows my thoughts and my heart, He knows that I love Him, and that gives me such a sense of peace."

I replied, "And God loves you so incredibly much, Dad, that He gave His Son for you, so you wouldn't have to die, but could live with Him!"

My dad said in response, "I know that Jesus died for me and that He is the Son of God, I truly believe that."

I couldn't believe what I was hearing! My father had just called Jesus his Redeemer! I saw his eyes glistening, and I knew: my father is saved. He may already have been saved when he had that moment with God all those years ago, but now he felt it deep in his heart!

From that time forward, almost all our conversations were about faith, and I knew: no matter what happens now, it will be good. The rest of the family also noticed that my father had changed a lot. He was much sweeter and softer.

A year after his recovery, he became very ill again, with a viral infection. It was clear that the end of his life was near, and that we should say goodbye while we still could.

He gave me his gold ring, which I had given to him as a present long ago, when I still cared about such things and had money to buy them. The ring had sentimental value, so I put it in a safe place. I rarely wore it, but it was very precious to me.

My father eventually slipped into a coma, and breathed his last breath a few days later, with all of us there in the house.

When my father's ashes were scattered at sea, someone read out loud a letter that he had written: "If you are hearing this letter, that means I have died." In the letter he talked about things that touched my heart: about my mother, about us, and how he had found his peace. Apparently, he had known he didn't have much time left, but he hadn't told anyone.

Such an extraordinary, strong man he had been! I was so proud to have him as my dad. When I thought of him now, it was always with joy, never with pain or regret. God had completely restored that relationship; that's how good He is. Now my dad was with the Lord, and that knowledge gave me so much joy. As the Bible says, "*whoever believes in Him should not perish but have everlasting life,*" John 3:16.

God's love and my desire to tell people about Him were having more and more of an impact on me as a person and on my behavior. By that point, the way I talked about Jesus had become less forceful and more driven by love for the people I was speaking to. Wouldn't it be cool if my brother[3] and our oldest daughter could also experience God's love? I wanted that so badly for them.

Seeing people's lives change through God's love: that was my passion. During my time at Bible school, I also looked for ways God might be able to use me for that purpose. Inspired by the teachings and the tools I was learning to use, I continued studying on my own and exploring the whole Bible in depth. I constantly asked myself: "God, what are You saying to me? How can You use me?"

Not long after, I was also allowed to start writing lesson materials and speaking at the school. Finding God had changed me immensely, and Brenda could see that too. A year later she also started attending Charis Bible College.

In addition to receiving and giving instruction, we also went out onto the street and talked to people about God's love. If people were in pain, we asked if we could pray for them, and usually they were fine with that. I wanted to do what the Bible said, and I experienced various miracles, hugely encouraging!

I was not the one making it happen, it was Him. There is only one Healer, and His Name is Jesus. I thought it was fantastic, and burned with a desire to see more miracles. Bring it on!

So I could hardly wait to go on a mission trip to Romania in my second year. Brenda went along too. In Romania we would be speaking in churches, organizing youth activities, and making house calls to the Roma.

The people there lived in extreme poverty. In spite of that, or possibly because of that, they were very open to God. I was in my element. I got to pray for lots and lots of people, and many of them were healed, and freed from demons.

In the Roma village we were planning to visit was a boy with a twisted back. He was about twelve years old and had been collecting wood almost all his life; they said that had caused his back to grow crooked. He was in a lot of pain.

The X-rays they sent to us clearly showed how twisted his spine was, just terrible. He really needed help, and they asked us to bring along a back brace for him.

Why would we do that? "We're not going to take along a back brace! We have Jesus with us, the Son of the Living God!" But that wasn't enough, apparently, so the back brace went along with us.

The brace was already in the back of our van when we drove to the boy's village. We visited about four other homes, dropped off care packages with food in them, and prayed for the people.

About an hour and a half later, our time was up, and we headed back to our hotel. Just before we drove out of the village, I saw a young boy with a twisted back standing in front of a house.

"Look, that's the boy we brought that back brace along for," said the Romanian driver who was working with us. "Would you like me to pull over?"

Enthusiastically, I said: "Definitely, pull over! We're going to pray for him!" "Should I bring along the brace?" he suggested helpfully.

"No, just leave it in the van," I said, filled with faith.

We walked over to the boy, and he invited us into his tiny home. There he stood, beside his mother: a boy who was literally bent over, pressed down by an enormous weight. Small, weak, and unable to develop into a strong, confident man.

AND AS YOU GO, PREACH,
SAYING, 'THE KINGDOM OF
HEAVEN IS AT HAND.'
HEAL THE SICK, CLEANSE
THE LEPERS, RAISE THE
DEAD, CAST OUT DEMONS.

MATTHEW 10:7-8

I wanted to start praying, "Back, in the Name of Jesus, be healed." But before I could speak the words, God said to me: "Do you remember that woman who had been bent over for eighteen years? She was pressed down by a spirit of infirmity. When Jesus set her free, she could stand up straight again. Send that demon away."

I was familiar with that story from Luke 13. I took hold of the boy, saying: "In the Name of Jesus, let him loose, now." The boy started sweating and fell to the ground, his limbs twitching. His mother started crying and wailing.

A few moments later the boy got up again. Straight as an arrow, he stood there before me, his shoulders relaxed; he was free! It had been demonic, and it was now broken!

I prayed the same for the wailing mother: "In the powerful Name of Jesus, be gone, Satan!" She also fell to the ground straight away, flailing around. A bit later, she got up and was calm again.

The driver and I looked at each other in amazement. What was going on here? Before our eyes and through our words, God was fighting with demonic powers, and setting these people free!

The woman came to faith then and there because she had seen and felt the power of God, and because her son had been healed. Their faces shone as bright as the sun. They hugged us over and over, so thankful for what had happened.

It was really amazing to be allowed to send demons away in Jesus' Name! This was a kickstart; I was on fire! From that moment on, I prayed for anyone who wanted it.

After the services where I spoke, lots of people came forward for prayer. I was tremendously encouraged, and proud that God was working through me to make it all happen. At the same time, I needed to stay humble. I myself wasn't doing anything at all; it was God working through us. No one should be putting me or anyone else on a pedestal.

In the past I had had a massive ego. Always wanted to be the biggest and the best. Thankfully, God made it clear to me from the start: it's not about Johan. Paul knew that too. He said, "*it is no longer I who live, but Christ lives in me,*" Galatians 2:20.

God works through everyone, with the same resurrection power. As the Bible says in Mark 16:17-18: "*And these signs will follow those who believe: In My name they will cast out demons; they will speak with new tongues,... they will lay hands on the sick, and they will recover.*" You only have to believe that He is willing and able to work through you.

That was the good news that I was privileged to preach: know who you are in Christ. Everyone has the power of God within them. We can all rise up and shine for His Kingdom. No one has an excuse.

GO THEREFORE AND MAKE DISCIPLES OF ALL THE NATIONS, BAPTIZING THEM IN THE NAME OF THE FATHER AND OF THE SON AND OF THE HOLY SPIRIT, TEACHING THEM TO OBSERVE ALL THINGS THAT I HAVE COMMANDED YOU.

MATTHEW 28:19-20

24

BRAZIL

Yelling and cursing, the man stomped after everyone who crossed his path. I could feel the tension around me and in me. On the one side, broken children in filthy rags who looked lost, no idea who they could trust or whether they would have food to eat that day. On the other side, the dealers, the alcoholics, the crackheads and the prostitutes.

It was a melting pot of insanity and godlessness. The tiny houses built from old stones, boards and plastic looked like they could collapse at any moment. Wrecked cars had been stripped of anything valuable. Dead rats, garbage and litter covered the streets.

My heart was pounding. I could feel the negative vibe in the air. It was now or never. All eyes were on me; I could feel people watching me, even from inside the houses and on the rooftops. What would I do? Should I go confront the man, or let it slide?

It was 2016. Brenda and I had gone on various missions trips together. We were increasingly discovering that this was what set our hearts on fire: going to places that other people preferred to avoid, making a difference in people's lives because of who we were as children of God.

Between trips, I sometimes taught Bible classes and spoke in churches or prisons. We both loved the work and were hugely encouraged by the miracles and conversions that we witnessed.

By that time our family and the people around us had grown used to our new lifestyle. We only got positive feedback. "You've both changed so much!" and "Just looking at you brings us joy! You're radiant and look so happy!"

That's how we felt, too! Every day we woke up feeling grateful for another new day in which we knew that we were loved and that we could walk with our God again. Even though we were far from perfect and still made mistakes, He saw our hearts and our desire to serve Him. We were complete in Christ, as Colossians 2:10 says. What a wonderful Father we had!

After four years of Bible school and mission trips, God pounded on my heart and said: "Onward. Onward." He wanted us to move on, do something else, and I felt that I wanted that too, although I wasn't sure what it would be.

Charis Bible College was happy with us and would have preferred for us to stay, but they supported us, even giving us their blessing to start our own ministry. God was very clear, and I wanted to follow Him. I was an evangelist to the core and wanted to spread my wings.

Of course I was radical and enthusiastic about this, too. "Brenda, God is calling me to serve Him, and we need to make that official. We need to set up a foundation and register it as a charity with ANBI tax-deductible status." If I was going to do this, I was going to do it the right way from the start. I didn't know anything about foundations, but something in me clearly showed that this was the way I should go.

Establishing a foundation costs three hundred euros. We were still working to pay off our debts, so I didn't have any money left over to start anything at all. Where would I get three hundred euros?

Suddenly I remembered my father's gold ring. I was sure he wouldn't mind if I used that ring to do some good in the world. I took the ring to the pawnshop and asked the owner how much he could give me for it. "Three hundred euros," he said. Wow, exactly the amount I needed!

Within a few weeks our non-profit was up and running: the One in Him Foundation. We planned to organize evenings all summer to teach people about who they are in Christ.

For the time being we were allowed to use the school building. We didn't have a network of our own yet, so we had to figure everything out and organize it all ourselves: arranging light and sound, making and handing out flyers; I even had to blow up the baptism pool myself and empty it again afterwards.

It takes some dedication to make something like this happen. We did it together, Brenda and I, paying for everything out of our own pockets, and doing it with love.

There were about fifty people there that first night, and it was great. We had the privilege of praying with lots of people, and five were baptized. I didn't get to bed that night until 3 a.m., but I didn't care; it was fantastic!

Even more people came the second night, and on the third night we reached nearly a hundred! We kept going, and more and more visitors came. It was an amazing summer, in which many people were baptized and equipped to live in Christ. That was the start of our work.

Everything happened so fast, and it was only possible because we were following God's lead.

At the same time my heart burned to go out into the world, to bring the gospel to people far away, and to support people who were poor. I said it often, because I wanted to share the desires of my heart, and words have great power.

Brenda knew it too. She asked me, "If you could choose any country, where would you want to go?"

Without hesitation, I said, "Brazil." I already knew what she would say. "I feel exactly the same way." Wow, that was cool!

Of course, I didn't just leave it there; I took action right away. We decided to backpack through Brazil for six weeks, traveling from church to church to see what God wanted us to do.

We had never been there before, and didn't know anyone in that country. Still, we were both convinced that we had to go. We told people that, too, even though we didn't know what would happen and didn't have any money to our names. It was going to happen; we were both sure of that.

We got contact details for someone in Brazil and spent a couple hours Skyping with her. Taking a pro-active approach, we started planning right away: not next year, but as soon as possible.

All summer long we collected money for our trip to Brazil. It was great to see that people were willing to support us in this, even if we didn't know ourselves yet what we were going to do there. Four people even decided to go along with us.

Eventually all the arrangements were made, and we were really going. I had no idea where we would end up, but we would see what happened. Our desire to go out into the world came from God, and so we went. Go forth! I took that calling very seriously!

Once we landed and left the airport, we both felt exactly the way we had felt in Romania: this was where we were supposed to be. We even spoke the language because of the time we had spent in Portuguese prisons. It seemed God had been preparing us for this even before we knew Him. Bizarre. It was a new adventure in our rollercoaster lives, but this time we were serving the Lord.

We ended up in São Paulo, where we would spend some time in the middle of a nature reserve. I could hear the monkeys hooting; parrots and enormous butterflies flew through the air; we were surrounded by the overwhelming beauty of nature: it was like paradise! We slept in an attic with no facilities: no beds, no doors for the toilets, nice and primitive. But we had great fun.

The owner, Alex, told us that people would meet at his place every so often to discuss all sorts of things, including faith. They were usually young people, and many of them had been disappointed by churches where the focus seemed more on keeping the commandments than on truly loving God and other people. As a result, they often felt a sense of condemnation, like they weren't good enough. Oh, how well I knew that one.

We immediately knew that God wanted to bring restoration to this place. We stayed there for three days, and it felt great. They asked us if we wanted them to accompany us to the nearby slums, to a *favela*, and if I would be willing to give my testimony right there on the street, in the middle of the *favela*. That was a big deal for me!

I had never been in such a poor neighborhood before, but I knew all the stories: people were murdered there on a daily basis, and violence, prostitution and crime were nonstop. That was my impression, and I wasn't thrilled at the idea of going there.

The morning before we were to head out, I walked up the mountain near where we were staying to spend some time talking to my Father. "Lord, if it is Your will for me to do this, then I will do it. I will not be afraid, and I will trust You completely. Even though it might cost me my life, I will go there for Your Kingdom and to tell them about Your love. Thank You for protecting me from the darkness of that place with an army of Your angels. Here I am, Lord. Send me, and use me to glorify Your Name. Amen." Now I was ready to go.

Once we got to the *favela*, I saw that it was a huge mess. Tiny houses built from boards, stones and assorted rubble leaned against each other, looking like they could collapse at any moment. Children ran barefoot through the streets, which were covered in dog poop, garbage and broken glass. They had to watch where they walked so they wouldn't step on used drug needles.

Loud music blared from every corner, all sorts of music at the same time. People were shouting and drinking in the middle of the road, while cars drove through the narrow streets, honking the whole time. Big tangles of power cables hung over our heads. The high-voltage cables ran right over the *favelas*, and made the situation incredibly dangerous.

There were huge dead rats on both sides of the street, probably poisoned, and no one bothered to clean them up. In the middle of the street drug addicts were smashing old household appliances and wrecked cars. It was a familiar sight, seeing addicts compulsively doing pointless activities. That's what crack does to you. But this was extreme.

The junkies sat around using together, looking strung out under a homemade tent put together from random trash. Sometimes they would shout at each other aggressively with children playing around them, unbothered by the conflict. I saw various street dealers selling their product openly, right where we could see. It was a well-oiled machine; I knew the movements and the looks all too well. It was pure darkness, and it made my skin crawl, because it was so exactly the opposite of what God intended for these people.

I remembered what Jesus said: *"The thief does not come except to steal, and to kill, and to destroy. I have come that they may have life, and that they may have it more abundantly,"* John 10:10. Brenda could barely hold back her tears; our hearts wept for these people.

We had brought a couple of clowns along with us. Dozens of children shouted happily as the clowns did a song and dance and handed out balloons. Their little faces beamed, but I could see trauma and suffering behind their smiles. Brokenness.

These children were deeply damaged. So much love and attention were needed here. And there was so much practical work that could be done! If only I was a millionaire again, I could rebuild the whole *favela* and create jobs for these people.

My train of thought was abruptly interrupted when someone tapped me on the shoulder and said, "It's time; you're up." The man handed me a microphone, and it was up to me.

Nervously, I looked around me and started telling my story. The whole situation felt pretty threatening. I prayed under my breath: God, this is Your witness, please speak through me and touch them. The people seemed to want to hear it and stuck around to listen. A bus full of people even stopped to hear what I had to say.

One man was very disruptive and aggressive. He was running after people like he was crazy; his behavior felt very threatening. I kept on talking anyway, hoping that he would stop. Meanwhile, people were dealing drugs right under my nose. I was familiar with that kind of provocation, and I didn't like it. The situation wasn't improving, so I prayed, "God, turn the mood around, in Jesus' Name; the darkness must give way now."

Then God suddenly said to me, "Go to that aggressive man and give him a hug." Wait, what? That crazy guy? Now? That wasn't exactly what I had in mind. In the middle of these slums, surrounded by drug dealers, addicts and criminals, I'm supposed to hug that aggressive guy? I stood hesitating for a moment, the tension soaring, all eyes on me. But... it is no longer I who live, but Christ in me. All right, if You say so...

As the people glanced a bit uneasily at the man, I said into my microphone, "What does it cost us to walk over to someone and give him a hug? Aren't we brothers and sisters?" The people looked at me in surprise, and I understood it.

My heart pounding, I walked over to the aggressive man, who looked at me warily. I laid my hand on his shoulder and gave him a hug. And as I stood there embracing him for a moment, it was like the heavens opened and the darkness was chased away. The whole atmosphere seemed to change; everything felt lighter now!

During the embrace, I had felt a large lump on the side of the man's body. Without hesitation, I started praying for it. Straight away he began to cry. He was touched by the love and compassion I gave him, clearly not common around here. A few minutes before, he had been running around screaming, and now he had been touched and he had been healed!

Encouraged, I walked back to where I had been standing and said, "I'm going to lay down my microphone now. Come to me if you need prayer. The Kingdom of God is here."

Like they had just been waiting for me to say that, people crowded toward me, and they all had just two requests: "I need healing, and could I also get a hug?" Wow! People were literally being touched; I could see the Holy Spirit at work, and wonderful signs and miracles were taking place.

This was where I wanted to be, surrounded by these people. Just like in Romania, I was in my element. My heart wept with joy! The world viewed these people as the lowest of the low, the scum of the earth. But these were people God wanted to share His love with, through me.

I had the privilege of hugging the filthiest people on the street. For someone who is rejected by everyone, God's love is even more important. They were able to feel human again, loved by other people and by God.

Brenda's face shone too, as she stood there hugging people and giving them encouraging words from God. Many tears rolled down the cheeks of those men and women. Brenda and I glanced at each other and clearly saw in each other's eyes: this is our calling. We wanted to give hands and feet to God's love, in word and in deed.

After a long afternoon filled with hugs and prayer, healing and liberating, and taking dozens of selfies, we ended up back at Alex's house. The adrenaline was coursing through my body; I was completely hyper and wound up. I could have gone on for weeks, that's how good I felt. What a great manifestation of God's love and His Kingdom! Enthusiastically, we discussed what had happened, and I gradually started calming down a bit.

Once I had landed a bit God said to me, "Go walk across the plot of land beside Alex's house." By that time I knew that God sometimes told me to do strange things that turned out to be exactly what needed to happen. Even so, at that moment I really had no idea what He was planning. I couldn't see anything but trees. What was I supposed to do there? So I went and asked Alex what that land was.

"Nothing is being done with it," he told me. "It belongs to those people down the road. I think it's for sale, but the owners are hardly ever there, so it would be difficult to make any arrangements."

I still had no idea why I had to walk over there, but I was still following along obediently, and more than a little curious.

"Bren, come," I said to her.

"What are you going to do?"

"God is calling."

Once we were on that plot of land, I walked in circles through the bushes, repeating over and over, *"Every place on which the sole of my foot treads shall be the territory of the Kingdom of God."* God had apparently put those words from Deuteronomy 11:24 in my mind, so I kept saying them aloud.

Brenda was standing along the edge. She thought I was crazy and definitely didn't want to walk with me. "What an idiot!" she mumbled to herself.

"I heard that!" I called to her, calmly continuing my walk – and feeling a little silly.

After a while I stopped and told Alex that I needed to talk to the owners. He didn't think it would actually work, but I persisted. I hadn't just walked all those circles for nothing, right?

Suddenly, I had an amount of money in mind. BAM. So that meant we had to buy it. I pressed harder, insisting that I needed to go speak with the owners.

In the end we went there. After we rang the bell three times, the gate opened. The owner was home, and she told us they were not only major landowners, but also Christians.

"How big is that plot of land, and would it be possible for me to buy it and build on it?" I asked her.

No idea why we would need to have that plot of land. I was just doing what God told me.

She pointed out the plot of land on the map. She told me it was for sale, and stated an amount that was twice what I had received in my mind. I looked at her for a moment, and then said, "Are you sure? Because God told me a very different amount." She was silent for a moment, looking out the window and contemplating. Then she turned back to me and stated exactly the amount that I already had in mind. "It's yours for this price." It was half the original amount! And exactly the price I had in mind, although she couldn't have known that. This was great!

"Thanks! One little problem: we don't have the money yet. But we really do want the plot of land!" Talk about trusting God. Really nerve-wracking, but I went ahead and did it!

The woman had to think about it again for a moment, but then she said, "If you make a down payment and then pay the rest in monthly installments, you can have it."

We had a deal! In a country I didn't know well, where I knew almost no one, we were buying a plot of land for the foundation, without knowing what it was for, and without having the money to buy it. Who does that?!

Alex thought it was fantastic, and was having grand ideas about our future collaboration. "We've been to the *favela* together once, but it would be great if we could do that together more often!"

He truly had a heart for the poor and the broken. Together, we could do so much more than he had managed to achieve on his own so far.

Ideas slowly started taking shape in my mind, and I shared them with Brenda. "I feel like God wants to build a mission house here where we can equip people and take them out on mission trips. We need to tell people in the Netherlands about it, and ask them to donate money for that plot of land."

Brenda was also enthusiastic. It was so extraordinary, the way we were developing the same desires and were able to do more and more together.

We went back to the Netherlands and organized a gathering. Super exciting. "God, You tell me I'm supposed to be doing this, so the money for it needs to be provided!" We told people about our plans, and that same night we raised the amount for the down payment, plus pledges from partners to pay the rest of the monthly installments. Fully provisioned in a single evening!

Our mission also needed a van; transport was a real problem. The foundation didn't have any money of its own yet, so buying our own van wasn't an option. We were going to have to ask for help. Surely there must be people who would be willing to help, through prayer, but also by making a financial contribution. And if I didn't tell anybody we needed it, no one would know and no one be able to help. So everywhere I went, I told people about it. "I'm truly not asking for myself; we need the van for the foundation. It'll save us a lot of money."

Someone came to us and said, "God has laid it on my heart to help you buy a van, so I'd like to give you a donation of twenty thousand euros." Praise God, we could buy a really nice van for that much money!

But God had other plans. That night I dreamed about a really cool new van. Then I heard God's voice: "Do you really need a brand-new van, or could it just be a good van, and would you be satisfied with something slightly less fancy?"

Ouch. "Yes, of course, Father."

We found a van for twelve thousand euros, and it was more than fine. I went back and told our generous donor that I wasn't going to need twenty thousand euros after all, but twelve. The fact that I told him honestly and didn't just cash in on the whole amount he had offered, well, he just loved it.

Later, because of that, he gave us a large sum of money to pay off our own debts. Thanks in no small part to that generous gift and God's supernatural provisions for us, we were completely out of debt and would be able to continue our work.

Several times a year, we took a group with us and traveled to Brazil. We visited slums and arranged all sorts of things for the children and their parents. We saw beautiful results. And we spent a lot of time among the homeless, visited the drug rehab clinics, and handed out food and clothing. We spoke of God's love and showed it in practice. In His Name we were able to work miracles.

We took the guys from the rehab clinic and headed out onto the streets to pray for people. So bizarre: first they had been addicts, rejected by everyone and everything, and never good enough. Then they had come to faith and were set free and filled with power, with a new awareness of who they were in Christ. And now they were heading out onto the streets to pray for others. They looked at us in surprise. "Are my sins truly forgiven? Can I also pray for other people?"

Jesus says, "*He who believes in Me, the works that I do he will do also; and greater works than these he will do* (...)," John 14:12. That was our vision: teach these men to fish. We passed that vision on to others and trained them to do the work there. And over and over, in miraculous ways, new people joined us.

Brenda had been saying for a while, "We should go visit Roberta sometime." Her friend was Brazilian, but we had met her when she was living with her husband and child in a down-market one-room apartment in Portugal. We had helped her start her own little shop.

She knew our past history all too well, all the drugs and crime. And of course she had seen our arrest on the news. In the end, she'd had to return to Brazil because her husband had left her and spent all their money.

We hadn't seen her in years, and I wasn't sure I wanted to meet her again and be reminded of our past. But Brenda persisted. She still had occasional contact with the woman and her daughter, and she really wanted to bring them to our project. "You never know what'll happen."

That was true, and yet I wasn't sure. On one of my walks, I asked God what I should do about it, and He said, "You should have her come here." That was clear enough.

We paid for her flight – Brazil is a very big country – and it was fantastic to see her again after all that time. We greeted each other with hugs, got all caught up, and were soon back on familiar footing. She came and sat with us when I told the people how God sees them and what we were going to be doing for the next fourteen days. This was completely new to her, of course; she had never seen us like this before.

Suddenly, she started crying! Her daughter was also very emotional. "I want what you guys have!" she said.

"Okay, you can have this too," I told her. Now I knew why she was supposed to come to us.

Over the course of an hour, I explained the gospel to them. I told them how God could come into their lives. In that moment, they gave their hearts to Jesus. They were baptized with water and in the Holy Spirit. Right away Roberta started helping out – translating, praying for people, and helping wherever she could. Such dedication!

God was adding the right people to the project. Wonderful things kept happening and He transformed people's lives completely. Time and time again, groups traveled from the Netherlands to Brazil.

The people who came were all Christians, and yet they also sometimes struggled with traumas from their past, rejection, or other types of pain. Many of them went home changed, with new insights into God's love and what He says in the Bible.

Over and over, we showed people that God loved them unconditionally. That they were good enough. I had already been writing about that in the diary I kept during my time in prison; as I read later, "God loves me unconditionally, and there is nothing I can do or fail to do that would make Him love me any more or any less."

You don't have to earn God's love. You're good enough. That was the message we wanted to bring to Brazil, and all over the world.

In essence, I still need to say that to myself every day.

GOOD ENOUGH

On a mission trip to the slums

I SHALL NOT DIE, BUT LIVE, AND DECLARE THE WORKS OF THE LORD.

PSALM 118:17

25

NEARLY DEAD, BUT NOT DEFEATED

Many churches in Brazil opened their doors to us. And I believed that was only the beginning of what God was going to do through our ministry. That was confirmed only more by the conflict we experienced. But at one point that conflict was nearly fatal for me.

On the first of January 2018, we said our goodbyes in Brazil to the group that we had been on a mission trip with. We had had two fantastic weeks and an unforgettable Christmas. Brenda and I stayed on another week to make arrangements for the mission trip in February. I had also been invited to speak in new churches.

We had done so much on this mission trip. First all the preliminary arrangements. Then buying and wrapping hundreds of Christmas presents and little outfits in the right sizes for the children. And organizing a huge party with all sorts of fun activities, including food for all the children and their parents. We had also visited clinics, given training courses, and preached. We had put together packages of food and handed them out, brought food and clothing to the homeless, and equipped the whole group.

It had been a packed program, and by then we were pretty tired. Still, we had enough energy to do just a bit more for His Kingdom. So we went back and visited the hundreds of homeless people again, handing out sandwiches, drinks and fruit, and praying for them.

The evening before we were to leave for the Netherlands, I was scheduled to give one more talk in a congregation I hadn't visited before. They had announced on social media and on their website that I would be coming, and were looking forward to having me there.

I was also looking forward to sharing God's great news with them. And I was looking forward to the signs and wonders that God would give us. As He said in the Bible, *"And they went out and preached everywhere, the Lord working with them and confirming the word through the accompanying signs. Amen,"* Mark 16:20.

It was around noon, and Alex and I were talking about the upcoming mission trip. The wind was blowing hard outside; it was cold out, and it had been raining for days. Every now and then, the blazing sun would break through briefly, but then vanish again behind the clouds.

I suddenly felt very cold and told Alex that I was going to go lie down for an hour to make sure I'd be well rested for the evening. When I got back to my room, I was talking to Brenda for a few minutes when my body suddenly started shivering all over. My teeth were chattering and I felt chilled to the bone.

Brenda said, "You're just cold, go lie down under the blankets." But I knew it wasn't just a chill, because I never felt the cold all that intensely. Even so, I crawled under the blankets and tried to get some sleep.

When I woke up, I felt pretty miserable. I spoke health over my body and blamed it on a minor cold, nothing to worry about. After a hot shower I got ready to go. I still felt far from fantastic, and I was getting worse and worse. Satan didn't want me to preach tonight, I thought. He wanted me to lose my focus and make sure these people wouldn't hear the truth about God's unparalleled grace and love. Well, he was out of luck. Even if I had to crawl there on my hands and knees, I was going to preach!

Once I was on the stage, everything seemed fine. I preached my heart out, and it was a great evening. When I called people forward, a hundred people came forward for prayer. I prayed for everyone and many were healed and set free. People were also baptized in the Holy Spirit. It was great, and I was in my element.

Once the last two people had had their turn for prayer, I felt myself shivering again, and could hardly control the spasms. Those people may have thought that it was God's Spirit working through me, because they started shivering and shaking along with me.

Once I had wrapped things up, I wanted to leave as soon as possible, because I was feeling worse and worse. I barely made it to the car, and when we got there, I sprawled in my seat and could hardly speak. I was vomiting and felt deathly ill.

After driving for two hours, I thanked God that we had arrived back at the project so I could go to bed. I hardly slept at all that night, and felt even worse the next day.

Alex suggested going to a doctor or hospital, but I resolutely refused. I'm absolutely not opposed to doctors, praise God that they're there, but I don't go running to a doctor for every cut or sniffle. First and foremost, I run to my Healer, Jesus, even when I can barely walk. But things were so bad that it was looking like I wouldn't be able to fly home that day.

Brenda tried to move heaven and earth to switch the tickets to a different day, but I decided to just head home anyway. Feeling the way I did, I preferred to be at home instead of in a foreign country. We decided to risk it.

After everything was packed, Alex took us to the airport, looking very worried. It was just a matter of praying and waiting to see if I could manage to make it onto the plane without throwing up all over everything. It was probably just a flu; it would be fine, really.

During the fourteen-hour flight, I thankfully had hardly any symptoms, and I thanked God for His goodness. "It's already almost over," I said. "See, no problem."

But I spoke too soon. As soon as I set foot outside the Dutch airport, the shivers came back as strong as ever. I constantly felt like I had to throw up. I hadn't eaten anything since Sunday and by then it was Tuesday, so nothing came up. But the nausea persisted, and I felt really terrible. We headed home as fast as we could; I wanted to go to bed. I was sweating buckets because of my high fever, and I kept shivering and feeling like I had to vomit.

By Wednesday morning, I was completely out of it. I couldn't communicate normally anymore and felt incredibly sick. I cursed Satan and all his tricks and praised God that He was still with me even now. He was my only comfort. I knew that, no matter how sick I felt.

On Wednesday evening I spent more than 30 minutes hanging over the toilet bowl, and suddenly I developed severe heart palpitations. They were so intense that I thought I was having a heart attack. Completely out of breath, I crawled to the couch, although I could hardly move normally anymore. Then I crawled over the floor back to the toilet. I had never been so sick in my life; I really felt like I was dying. God, what is happening to me?

I had lost a lot of weight. Not necessarily a bad thing, after gaining nearly fourteen pounds from all that delicious food in Brazil. But I was shedding weight so quickly there would be nothing left of me.

By then Brenda was seriously worried and urged me to go see a doctor. My heart was pounding wildly, and I realized something was seriously wrong with me, so I gave in and let her make an appointment.

On Thursday morning – by then I had been sick for four days – Brenda half-carried me into the doctor's office. I barely managed; I could hardly stand on my own two feet, so they let me lie on a bed in a separate room until the doctor had time to see me. It seemed to take forever.

Finally, a doctor came to us; after asking a few questions he immediately referred me to the hospital for tropical diseases in Rotterdam. Brenda drove us there, and I could only think: where's my bed? I want to lie down!

Again, I had to answer a lot of questions before I was put in a wheelchair and brought to a different building. Because I was so sick, at first they didn't want to take blood samples. The lady even wanted to call an ambulance to take me to the emergency room. "Never mind, just take the sample," I mumbled. And please hurry, I thought to myself.

In the end she agreed to do it. Then I had to go back to the other building. I was exhausted by then. Once I was back in the first building, they decided they also needed a urine sample, so off I was to the lab again. I felt like a yoyo. They were very concerned and wanted to exclude every possibility, so I didn't protest; I just let them do what they had to.

After I gave a urine sample and returned to the first building, a doctor came to see me. They hadn't gotten all the results back, but he suspected it was typhoid fever. I had heard of typhoid before; the disease was a common swear word in Dutch because it sounded so awful. That wasn't so terrible; I would be given some medicine and allowed to go home, and the doctor told me I would be better soon. Finally I could go back to my bed.

We were by the car and just about to drive away when a nurse came running. She had a wheelchair with her and said, out of breath: "Mr. Toet, could you please come back inside? It may be something else after all."

Brenda and I looked at each other. What else could it be? Worried, we went back inside. The doctor asked me to let them check me into the hospital, so they could examine me thoroughly. I wasn't happy with the idea; I hated hospitals.

"Just do it," Brenda said. "It's better if they really figure out what you have. I'm sure it will be over soon."

She was right, so I let them arrange a bed for me in the regular hospital. Then she went home and I was put in a two-person room. The man beside me was missing a leg; the wound was infected, and he was in a lot of pain. Through the curtain between our beds, I talked to him and told him that God loved him.

"I don't believe in God," he said.

"Oh, you don't have to believe in God for Him to love you. He already loves you, so there's nothing you can do to change that. It's too bad if you don't want to accept that love, but that doesn't change anything about His love for you."

"Well, those are positive words. Thanks, man!" He sounded a bit more cheerful than he had before.

"Thank God. It's Him who loves you, not me," I replied, and we both laughed.

I still wasn't sure why I was lying there; there were no doctors coming to check on me and they weren't giving me any medicine.

Toward evening, the man was suddenly taken out of my room. Then a doctor came and sat beside my bed looking very serious. She asked me to sit up and hold on tight to the edge of the bed, because she had very bad news for me. Surprised, I looked at her and pushed myself up.

Then she said, "Mr. Toet, you have yellow fever. There is a deadly virus in your body that's affecting your organs. They could start bleeding. You might turn yellow, and you could even die. We expect your condition to grow far worse. We are going to put you into quarantine as a precaution, and you're not allowed to leave your room at all. The doctors and nurses will have to wear protective suits and masks. It may seem unpleasant, but it's really necessary, because the virus could be very contagious."

She kept talking, explaining all sorts of instructions and actions to me, but the words didn't register. I replied in a friendly tone, "I'm not going to turn yellow, I'm not going to start bleeding, and I'm definitely not going to die, because my God has a hopeful future in store for me. I reject it all in the Name of Jesus. Nothing personal, doctor, I just believe in my God."

The doctor responded very calmly, and continued explaining that they would have to do lots of blood tests, and that they would be examining all my organs and so on. I would have to take a little pill for my extremely fast heart rate, and the rest would be a waiting game, she told me. "We can't do anything for you; there's no medicine for this." Sure there is! Jesus is my Physician!

Once the doctor was gone, I called Brenda and asked her not to tell anyone else, just to pass the news on to a few friends so they could pray for me. She was very worried, but I told her that everything would work out.

That evening, she came to visit me. She was feeling pretty sick herself; there was a good chance that she had food poisoning. Satan had targeted us both.

After I had said goodbye to Brenda and waited until it was less busy and the doctors and nurses weren't around, I sat on the edge of my bed and focused my thoughts on God. "Father, You know everything that they said about me today, but I spoke out against all of it, because You have a hopeful future for me. I know that You will fulfill Your promise." You said, "You shall not die, but live."
You said, "By My stripes they are healed."
You said, "I want to give you a future and a hope."
You said, "Fear not, for I am with you."
You said, "Trust in Me, I will never leave you nor forsake you."
You said, "Rejoice, and again I said rejoice."

"Dear Father, I believe what You have said, and I praise Your Name. Even if I die, You are good. I want to thank You for the wonderful time I have been able to have with my family, and the amazingly powerful things I have had the privilege of seeing You do. You have been good to me, are still good to me, and will always be good to me, no matter what happens. I love You and I know that this is not Your will. I place myself in Your hands. In the Name of Jesus, I rebuke the yellow fever and any other virus, any other bacteria, or whatever might be attacking me from the darkness. I speak health, strength and recovery in the Name of Jesus, and I am not afraid. I will live, in Jesus' Name!"

As I spoke those words, I felt a sense of peace and calm wash over me that were not of this world. And I knew for sure: I was healed.

The next morning, the doctors came to my bedside again and I told them that I was healed. One of the doctors happened to be a Brazilian woman, and I could speak Portuguese with her. "*Estou curado, Deus es bon!*" "*I am cured, God is good!*"

She smiled at me and said, "Well, we'll see about that. If your blood results and so on go up again, that would be good, but this virus comes and goes. You might think: I'm all better, and then it will come back even worse a bit later."

She wasn't scaring me; I calmly replied, "No, it won't. Jesus has healed me." She didn't argue; she told me that she still wanted to do all sorts of tests, and asked if I would be willing to see a number of doctors. "You're only the second patient in thirty years to come back to the Netherlands with yellow fever, and they're eager to see such a unique case."

I was in a supremely good mood, so I said, "Sure, no problem, let them come." Meanwhile I was thinking: there's nothing to see! I don't have yellow fever at all anymore! The day before I hadn't been able to talk, walk or think clearly. Today I was sitting up straight and grinning from ear to ear. The doctors I saw were very surprised, because they had never encountered a God like mine before.

That evening my family came by with some friends. My good friend prayed that my pulse rate would go down and that I would recover quickly. I witnessed to the nurses, the doctors and anyone who dropped by about how I had been healed.

On Sunday, I packed up my things and set them aside to take home with me, although the doctor had said that it wasn't yet certain that I could go home. However, my blood results were ridiculously good and everything seemed to be just fine. I was absolutely sure. I thought to myself: I'm cured. Just heart palpitations, but other than that I felt a hundred percent better.

On Monday morning, the two doctors who had been handling my case since Thursday came to tell me that I could go home. "It's truly a miracle that you recovered so quickly. There has been an outbreak of yellow fever in the area you visited. Hundreds of people have died of the virus."

Monkeys could carry the virus, so all the monkeys in the area had been killed, parks had been closed, and a total of 72 million people had been vaccinated against the lethal virus. The Brazilian newspapers and the evening news mentioned that a Dutch man had also caught yellow fever.

My story was also published in various newspapers and on social media in the Netherlands. The doctors even invited me to come speak at a conference, telling over six hundred doctors about how I had been cured. What an opportunity to glorify God!

Once I was back home and things had calmed down, I started processing what had happened. Now that my story had been picked up by the media, I felt very strongly that God wanted me to tell people about my healing and witness about His greatness and power.

I contacted a Christian media platform and shared my testimony over the phone. They posted a few sentences about my story on their website.

A few days later I started getting strange emails, and odd comments under the article on the site. Most of them were from people

I WILL PRAISE YOU,
O LORD, WITH MY
WHOLE HEART;
I WILL TELL OF ALL
YOUR MARVELOUS
WORKS.

PSALM 9:1

ridiculing me for saying that God had healed me. Predictable, I didn't care about that. They didn't know God, and there would always be mockers. They were attacking God, not me; God could handle that.

The responses that affected me most powerfully were a completely different matter. It turned out that there was another man named Johan Toet, who had been arrested in Brazil a long time ago for possession of child pornography, and was allegedly in hiding in the Netherlands. People were sending me threatening messages because they thought I was that man. Even though it wasn't true, people still thought: where there's smoke, there's fire.

I was pretty angry about that! It was damaging my good name, my integrity and the work of the foundation. How can you protect yourself from such ugly lies? My solid alibi – that I had been serving a prison sentence in Portugal during the time when that man had gone to Brazil – wasn't something I could easily post everywhere online. That was nobody's business.

People would understand that I wouldn't be visiting Brazil several times a year if I was *that* Mr. Toet, right? Apparently, they weren't making that connection.

Just great. Travel to the other side of the world to serve the Kingdom of God, give everything you have, get struck down by a deadly virus and survive it thanks to God's healing, witness about it to glorify God, and then get savagely attacked for something you haven't even done! Discouraged, I thought: get lost, all of you, and leave me alone. I quit. I don't want to deal with this.

Suddenly, I realized that was exactly what the devil wanted. He was attacking from a different angle, because his attack on my body hadn't killed me after all. He wanted me to toss my towel in the ring, to give up and walk away, to prevent what God had in store for my life.

I immediately got up and started rebuking the devil in the Name of Jesus. "Even if it costs me my life, I will never stop, because it is no longer I who live, but Christ in me. My answer in the face of fear is: 'I'm going to do it anyway!' Go away, you horrible serpent! I will keep going, no matter what you put in my path; every lie will be revealed. You will be exposed, devil! You cannot devour me!"

And to God, I said, "Lord, You know the truth. Let it be revealed in the light. You said, 'I will take care of your enemies; vengeance is Mine.' Lord, I lay it all in Your hands, I trust in You. In Jesus' Name, amen."

THE DEVIL WALKS ABOUT LIKE A ROARING LION, SEEKING WHOM HE MAY DEVOUR.

1 PETER 5:8

Two days after the emails, I received a call from a friendly investigative journalist from a major national newspaper in the Netherlands. The man told me he had been receiving all sorts of concerned phone calls and emails from people who thought that the person involved could move freely between Brazil and the Netherlands.

"When the case first came out, there were questions in Parliament about how this man could flee the country with the assistance of the Dutch embassy. It was an international scandal, which is why many people are so indignant now."

I understood completely. But what did I have to do with any of it? The journalist continued, "When I researched who you were, I immediately discovered that you weren't the person involved in that case. Different date of birth, different birthplace, and so on."

Well yeah, I could have told him that. Since it didn't have anything to do with me, he said he would notify those concerned citizens about the misunderstanding. After that, we ended the phone call.

Such a bizarre story; you couldn't even make it up! And all this because I had witnessed online about being healed after catching yellow fever in Brazil. Only Satan could cause such confusion, but 'the truth will set you free'.

After that, I received various email apologies from people who had accused me before. The persecution and conflict were over – for now. All glory to God who protects and guards me. For Him I would continue courageously, and let nothing and no one stop me from making Him known. Whatever it took.

In 2007 God had already said that I would write a book. In 2017 I shared my testimony on an *Hour of Power*, broadcast on Dutch National TV and viewed nearly half a million times, and I knew for certain: my story needs to be told.

Not because Johan is great, but because Jesus is great.

Not because I have the answers, but because He is the answer. Not for what I did, but for what He has done.

THE LORD IS NOT WILLING THAT ANY SHOULD PERISH BUT THAT ALL SHOULD COME TO REPENTANCE.

2 PETER 3:9

EPILOGUE
HIS HEART, MY HEART

God's unconditional love for people has taken hold of me. It is so pure and clean, so indescribable, so high that I cannot attain it, as David says in Psalm 139. I am willing to do anything for Him, and I feel a burning desire to tell people all over the world about this love, because I think everyone should have it.

God has called me to bring the gospel to many people, and I am eager to fulfill that calling. Looking back through my old diary, I came across this bit that I wrote in 2007: "I am deciding to serve God with my whole life, because He's the best boss you could ever imagine working for."

In my cell back then, I would pace back and forth and 'preach' out loud: "Dear people, have you already heard about the love of Jesus?" My heart burns with the fire of this calling.

The message I have to tell isn't a difficult theological story; it's simple. God gave His Son to save us, and that includes you! You'd just be crazy to turn that down.

Yes, it's a big step, but God says, "Just start, and the rest will follow." And I started. I have devoted my whole life to reading the Bible and telling others about His love.

Some people might think: that Johan, he's lost it. Yes, maybe. Others may think I'm arrogant. That's definitely not the case. This isn't about Johan, it's about God! God is great and He loves everyone. The whole world needs to know that.

God completely transformed and restored my life. This isn't some fairy tale, it's real life. If God is able to take such a profoundly broken, hardened life, drenched in darkness, and bring it into the light, to heal it and use it to glorify His Name, then He can do that with anyone's life!

Because: *"Jesus has come to save that which was lost,"* Matthew 18:11, and *"I will be a Father to you, and you shall be My sons and daughters, says the Lord Almighty,"* 2 Corinthians 6:18.

EYE HAS NOT SEEN,
NOR EAR HEARD,
NOR HAVE ENTERED INTO
THE HEART OF MAN,
THE THINGS WHICH GOD
HAS PREPARED FOR
THOSE WHO LOVE HIM.

1 CORINTHIANS 2:9

All the things God has done for me and for my family, I am sure He is willing to do them all for you, too. *"For God so loved the world –* not this one guy or that one girl, no, the world, and that means everyone *– that He gave His only begotten Son, that whoever believes in Him should not perish but have everlasting life,"* John 3:16.

It may seem so illogical, so distant, maybe not meant for you at all. Nothing could be farther from the truth. It's absolutely for you, and for anyone who feels lost in this world. If I could let you feel what I feel and see what I see, I would do that straight away.

If I could do that, I know for sure you wouldn't hesitate another second; you'd run straight into God's arms.

Take up the challenge and find out for yourself. Say these words from your heart: "God, if You are real, then I want to know You. Here I am." I said it too, when I was at the end of my rope.

And if you do know God, then read more about Him. Even if you haven't been called to become an evangelist, you have been called to be a disciple of Jesus and to follow in his footsteps. Read the Bible; truly get to know God. He has something far better in store for you than a sleepy Christian life.

Let your light shine to the glory of God, as it says in Matthew 5:16. He wants to raise you up to soaring heights and let you shine in your true destiny.

God is great and He loves you. That has nothing to do with the church or religion; it's a personal relationship between God and you. It doesn't matter if you've believed all your life, or strayed from the path, regardless of whether you lost your way because of circumstances, or by your own choice. God says, "My son, My daughter, I miss you and I want to give you everything."

Dear reader, it doesn't matter who you are, what you're doing now, or what you have already done. Through His Son Jesus, God has cleared the way for you to be able to come home again. God is saying to you: "You are good enough!"

I CHALLENGE YOU

If you've been touched by my story and by what God can do, and you'd like to give yourself to God, then pray the prayer that is provided below.

Please note: it's not about the words that you pray, but about the motivation of your heart. *"If you confess with your mouth the Lord Jesus and believe in your heart that God has raised Him from the dead, you will be saved. For with the heart one believes unto righteousness, and with the mouth confession is made unto salvation,"* Romans 10:9-10.

In other words, when you say these words, open your heart and believe in what you're saying. Then you will be born again and be accepted as His child.

The prayer:

"Father God, I come to You and ask You: forgive me.
I can no longer justify myself, and I don't want to anymore. I turn my back on my old life and give myself to Jesus. I believe that Your Son Jesus died for my sins and that You raised Him from the dead. I accept Jesus as my Savior and my Lord. Here I am, Lord, I give myself to You. Take my life and bring me back to my true destiny: to be Your beloved child.
I believe that I am now Your child, and that You will make me new again. In Jesus' Name. Amen."

Congratulations! You are now a child of God!

Welcome home!

AFTERWORD

To everyone I have harmed, I would like to say: I am sincerely sorry. I can no longer go back and change what happened; I can't give back what I took. I can say that my life now brings blessings instead of curses. The old Johan is dead as a doornail. *"It is no longer I who live, but Christ lives in me,"* Galatians 2:20. I pray to my Heavenly Father that you will discover God's love in your lives as well.

To everyone who stole from me, threatened, cheated, swindled, hurt or betrayed me, spit on me, damaged me, beat and kidnapped me, I would like to say: I have sincerely forgiven all of you, each and every one, with no exceptions.

I would also like to thank everyone who kept believing in me. Of course I'd particularly like to thank my wife Brenda, my precious angel, my ally and my best friend, without whom my life would have taken a very different direction. My darling, I am grateful that you never let me go, even if I often gave you more than enough reason to. I thank God for giving me one of the most beautiful gifts of my life, and that's you. I love you with all of my being. You deserve the very best. I want to grow old with you and conquer the world for His Kingdom. You are my true love.

I would like to thank my dear, sweet mother for her unconditional support and loving care in the darkest periods of our lives. You are a God-given gift to everyone who knows you. My respect and gratitude also go to my father, who is now with the Lord. Dad, I want you to know that I would not have wanted to have any other father here on Earth but you. I love you the way you were, and I am certain that we will see each other again!

I would like to thank my children for never holding anything against me and for making me feel like I'm good enough for them, as a father and as a person. Through you, I see His boundless goodness and love over and over. He gave you to me like gifts from heaven, bringing joy to my life each and every day.

I would also like to thank all the people who support us in the work that we do for His Kingdom, who have become our dear friends over the years. Each of you is precious, proof that good friends really do exist. I'd also like to thank all the leaders who worked with us and serve in unity in the Kingdom, and have given us a great deal of wise counsel.

Above all, I want to thank my Heavenly Father and give Him all glory and honor for everything He has done in my life. Father, I need You every day for my very existence. Without You, I am nothing, I can do nothing, I will always be nothing. But to You, I will always be good enough.

I will never forget where You found me.
The state I was in.
Broken, lost, fearful, lonely and empty.
I had no value for society; I was a burden and a curse.
I harmed other people and myself.
I was egotistical. Selfish. Focused on myself.
And You found me. Came to me.
Overcame me. Washed over me.
Transformed me. Saved me.
Now You shape me, mold me,
Cherish me, use me.
I thank You for this, praise You for it.

Because I will never forget where You found me.
I was nothing.
I had nothing.
I could do nothing.

But You fixed me.
Restored me.
Cared for me.
I am where I am today through You alone.

Let me never think that I am where I am by my own doing.
By my cunning. My knowledge.
My intelligence. My strength.
My wisdom. My character.